The Lady
Who Tamed
Pegasus

The Story of Pancho Barnes

Grover Ted Tate

— A MAVERICK PUBLICATION —

Copyright © 1984 by Grover Ted Tate
5th Printing 1989

ISBN 0-89288-092-9

Dedicated to my wife Cecilia Ramona, and to my children Cindy, Joe, Tedi, and Sara. They were sincere friends of Pancho's when she was in twilight.

INTRODUCTION

This is a love story about me and a lady called Pancho Barnes. It started in fantasy when I knew her only by reputation and endured in reality for more than thirty years. Only when the lady's stout heart gave in to the severe demands of its owner did the affair end.

Pancho carved her niche in flying history as a flamboyant pilot of the roaring twenties and depressed thirties. She did most of the things which women were supposed not to do and she did it with classic flair. As a good writer is supposed to write, Pancho lived her life; she told the world what she was going to do, she did it, and then told them what she had done.

As a young Air Corps officer I often stood on the sidelines at Pancho's Happy Bottom Riding Club near Edwards Air Force Base (then Muroc Army Air Field) in the Mojave Desert of California and envied all of those who were her friends. For many years I had heard stories of this fabled lady pilot and as I watched her bounce around the club, I instinctively knew that they were all true.

I was the classic aviation nut and loved every aspect of flying. The people involved in it were my heroes and Pancho was a very special hero because she was the outspoken maverick. She was the colorful, the unique, the "cock of the air." She was a varied weave of many talents; artist, writer, actress, dancer, deckhand, horsewoman, and a damned hot pilot.

I was an early-day admirer of Pancho but only a latter-day disciple of her life and legends. We were "pals" and for each of us life had served with excellent humor and extremely questionable judgment in that we elected to thumb our respective noses at society in general.

i

For the last ten years of her life I traipsed about with Pancho and her stories became a permanent part of my memory. We sat on corral fences, hiked about the arid desert, ate in greasy spoons, and roared around the desert in my hopped-up T-Bird with no top. We did the banquet circuit and we had a hell of a lot of fun. Together, we planned to do the book of her ribald and historic life but she filed her final flight plan before we could get it done. During those times when we tried to coax the dream of the book into reality Pancho gave me notes which were like the music that was background for the ticks of her spectacular but irregular career. This then, is a solo effort, born of that which we planned to do together.

Pancho is history and Pancho was fun. Not too many in history can make that claim. I loved Pancho for all that she was and didn't give a damn about those things she wasn't. I hope that I have presented her so that you will share that same admiration and understand the love.

As a prelude to the story of Pancho Barnes, I include a part of Pancho and me as it happened on a stage in Lancaster, California in April, 1975.

ME AND PANCHO

April, 1975
"Ya, you put your foot in your mouth, Buster. Bravo! Now what you gonna do?" she taunted.

She was right. Somewhere in the back of my being the ghost of Pancho Barnes had goaded me into making a perfect ass of myself before an audience of about two thousand people. Not just a Wednesday afternoon Garden Club audience, but one filled with heroes, stars, and important corporate officials. It was the annual get-together of a group of flying buffs dedicated to the preservation of historic aircraft.

This group created an Airplane Museum in the Mojave Desert of California and incorporated it as the Antelope Valley Aero Museum. To stimulate interest in the museum an annual banquet tagged "Barnstormers' Reunion" was

ii

begun and within six years had grown from an attendance of two hundred to two thousand. Guests included present and past greats of the entertainment and flying worlds, from Boots Le Boutellier, the last survivor of the flight during which the Red Baron was shot down, to Buzz Aldrin, the second man on the moon. Richard Arlen, whose movie *Wings* won the first Academy Award, was among the guests, as was Susan Oliver, the beautiful actress/flyer. Chuck Yeager, the first man to fly faster than the speed of sound was a member as was General Jimmy Doolittle and Astronaut David Scott. Batman was there and movie funnyman Vince Barnett was always a star of the show. Congressmen, corporate officials, Astronaut (General) Bob Rushworth, Space Shuttle Launch Pilot Fitz Fulton, test pilots Tony Le Vier and Fish Salmon were there and movie parachutist Bob "Redbeard" Sinclair escorted beautiful Tiny Broadwick, the first lady of parachuting. It was a damn interesting group of people.

From the very sparse beginning of this barnstorming program I was the master of ceremonies for the banquet. I had so many talented people to work with that it had to be a success. Pancho Barnes and I had an act—I would introduce her with only subtle references to her intellectual and sometimes raunchy background. She would recite a bit about her early flying days and then tell an outrageous, profane, obscene, and hilarious story. I would act surprised and shocked and we always left them laughing.

After six years of this buffoonery, the officials of the Museum decided that we needed less fun and more dignity. I as President, did not agree but was outvoted. No more dirty stories by Pancho, no profanity; decorum and dignity instead. I relayed the ridiculous decision to Pancho.

"Fuck 'em all," she growled.

"Most of those pious sons of bitches come to that asinine meeting to listen to my stories, not to hear about a fucking financial report. Tell 'em that I won't be there and they'll stay away in droves," she added.

Pancho was irate and I tried to soothe her.

"They want you to be there and to make a talk, but they

just don't want you to use any profanity," I pleaded with her.

"O.K., that's a deal. No profanity, not one goddamn word of profanity," and her eyes sparkled like the Fourth of July.

"You just do your usual act with the introduction then get the hell out of my way and I'll go from there. I know just the story for those stupid assholes," Pancho told me.

"Nope. Not unless you tell me the story first and I decide whether it's acceptable to the Board," I told her.

"O.K., Mr. Big Shot Board Member. I'll tell you a story," and she did.

She saw the shock on my face and she was delighted.

"Gotcha. No fucking bad words. Just nice everyday grammar school nouns and verbs and stuff. Not too many adverbs, a minimum of adjectives and not a single sentence is immoral enough to end in a preposition," she bragged.

"No way, no, no way are you going to tell that story, Pancho! Profanity or not, it won't do," I told her.

"O.K., O.K., you tell those assholes that you gave me the message and that I'll accept the invite and that I will behave," she instructed. Then she winked wickedly, "Not like the good old days."

I knew that I had been had, but I was always on Pancho's side and would enjoy the con as much as she. Dutifully I told the Board of the decision, leaving out the story, and all seemed well satisfied. Plans and publicity for the big shindig went ahead full-bore.

A week before the scheduled "dignified" meeting, Pancho's heart gave out and she died, tragically alone. She would tell no more ribald stories to a mortal audience but would probably rendezvous with some of her old buddies who didn't give a damn whether she used profanity or not. The planned reunion was changed to a testimonial wake for Pancho.

As the huge room filled with people, I felt a sadness that was overwhelming. Without Pancho, the fun was gone and no matter what the night might bring, the event would be hollow and without meaning. When General and Mrs. Jimmy Doolittle arrived, I told him of the story that Pancho was going to tell and asked if he thought it approriate for me

iv

to tell it. He vetoed the idea but told me that we must sometimes do those things which we as individuals think to be best. I decided against the story.

After the meeting was launched, General Doolittle gave a sentimental but realistic eulogy for Pancho. A toast to her was offered, and she was put to rest—but not quite!

The scheduled program dragged, a drunken stand-up comic from Las Vegas was laying bombs, the hour was growing late, and the audience was both sleepy and restless. The entire evening was becoming a dismal failure.

Mabye I wished it, or dreamed it, or made it up, or had too much to drink, but I felt Pancho's presence and she demanded my attention.

"Hook that guy off the stage and take over the show. You've got the balls to wake 'em up and get some fun out of this dull, fucking mess. Tell 'em a story, like maybe you heard one lately that they'd like," she whispered.

"Yeah, like one you told me, eh?" I teased.

"Yeah, something like that. Just be real careful not to talk dirty," and she laughed.

Drink, imagination, and perhaps a desire to see Pancho's con through to the finish conspired and like Red Skelton's "Mean Little Kid," I flashed a mental "I dood it."

The comic was ushered from the stage and I put my hands on the sides of the rostrum, bowed my head, and things became very quiet. Perhaps they expected a sermon. As dramatically as I knew how, I told of Pancho's plan to tell a special story—a story like only she could tell. I added that Pancho had told me that story. The audience grew hushed. Although Pancho was no longer there, my part of the act was still working.

"I know it's late, we're all getting tired and a little drunk, but would you like to hear Pancho's story?" I asked.

The old North Carolina Medicine Man scam worked its magic and there was a roof-rattling, spontaneous roar of "Yes!"

The story:

A middle-class suburban housewife had an overwhelming compulsion for buying shoes and a corresponding habit of never wearing a brassiere or under panties. This combination caused her to be the owner of more shoes than she could ever wear and to be the target of shoe salesmen's salacious stares and suggestive remarks.

Her husband tolerated this strange behavior for awhile but finally put his foot down. He forbade her from buying shoes and he insisted she wear panties.

All went well for awhile until the day when she succumbed to her strange habit and fell from grace. When her husband got home that fateful evening, he found her sitting on the living room floor, surrounded by new shoes and sobbing uncontrollably.

"You did it again," he accused.

"Yes, but it was worse this time," she sobbed. "A salesman really insulted me."

"How?" the husband inquired sarcastically.

"He looked up my dress and said that my thing was so pretty that if it was filled with peach ice cream that he could eat every bit of it," she wailed.

The husband laughed.

"Well, aren't you going down there and defend my honor? I should think you would want to beat that smart aleck unmercifully," she continued.

"Nope. No way. For two reasons. One, you didn't keep your promise, and two, there is no way that I'm going to start any kind of a fight with a guy who is big enough to eat that much ice cream," the husband concluded.

The applause pegged the meter but within minutes a tight knot of grim-faced directors descended upon me and demanded my resignation.

I apologized to General Doolittle and he told me that he did not agree with what I had done, but as he had said previously, if we all agreed on everything, we would be pretty dull people.

The morning following this indiscretion, Pancho's son, Bill, and I scattered the ashes of her remains over the site of her "Happy Bottom Riding Club."

As the ashes floated to the desert earth below, I could hear Pancho chuckling all the way down.

She sat on a raven black mustang on the rim of the steep-walled red canyon. She was alone.

Her face was as deeply etched with lines as the arroyos of the canyon that stretched before her. As with a good cowhide, her face had been tanned by the sun and the wind. Some of her face had yielded to time, but her chameleon eyes sparkled with their secret knowledge that they belonged to someone very special. On this particular evening they were unusually bright, for a new adventure waited to unfold before them.

Her black hair, fugitive from the graying of the years, was tied by a bloodred band of cloth with glistening silver conchos at the temples. The band crossed her wide forehead between flat eyebrows and curved hairline. She squinted into the dying sun and the conchos of her headband glowed orange with the reflected rays of the sun.

A toga-like garment of buffalo skin hung from her shoulders and reached to her knees. Her bare arms and legs were deceptively small, making her look like a diminutive warrior on the magnificently-muscled mustang.

She wore light colored, heavily-beaded moccasins, and a string of bright feathers trailed from her ankles.

Her horse was the classic horse of the warrior, black as a canyon on a moonless night and muscled so tightly that it seemed he might burst through the shiny coat. His nostrils flared and his eyes rolled as impatience overcame discipline. He had no saddle and the reins were of hand-braided hides.

The hands holding the reins were dainty with long, well-manicured nails painted a bright crimson. The hands fumbled nervously with the reins and fingered a spear held beneath an arm.

She watched the canyon floor below where cowboys were building a campfire and a cook was starting to fix supper. She watched directors, producers, grips, makeup people, script girls, cameramen and actors as they scurried about like frenzied pack rats.

As the sun slipped out of sight, she trembled a bit for the evening was growing cold. She dug the blunt end of the spear into the ground and shifted impatiently on her mount.

"What are those assholes doing?" she mumbled to herself. "A couple of years ago I could have bought and kept all of those incompetent sons of bitches. Wish I had, and I'd show those weenies how to really make a picture," she continued thinking out loud.

"What the fuck am I doing here anyway? A sixty-five year-old broad, nearly naked and freezing her tits off, waiting to ride this racehorse down the side of a cliff. For a lousy $65, that's what the fuck I'm doing here, because I need the fucking lousy $65," she now spoke in a louder voice, but only the horse could hear her.

She scanned the scene below and to take her thoughts away from the increasing chill of the night, she thought of other movies and of other days when she gave car parking boys bigger tips than $65!

Florence Leontine Lowe, alias Pancho Barnes, now just an old woman on a horse playing like an Indian. She waited for a signal to start on a wild ride down the hill and through the camp where she was to plant a flaming spear among the camping cowboys.

She waited and dreamed. Dreamed of a day when she didn't have to put up with this kind of shit.

* * *

Florence Leontine Lowe was born into American royalty on July 29, 1901 and she roared, under the astrological sign of Leo, from that day on. Her home was a 32-room mansion in San Marino, California, the elegant San Marino of the days before the real estate thieves and *nouveaux riches* got their hands on it. She came into a life of ease, of turn-of-the-century style, when grace and proper manners prevailed.

Her paternal grandfather was Professor Thaddeus S.C. Lowe, one of the founders of the California Institute of Technology (then known as Throop College of Technology), an inventor, and a visionary who got things done. Professor Lowe built hot air balloons during the Civil War era and used them as reconnaissance posts for the Union armies. Commanding a cadre of fifty men, Lowe sailed over the countryside to plot the positions and strengths of the Confederate troops. The information gleaned during these flights would be relayed to Union Headquarters to be used for battle plans. United States Air Force, Civil War style!

After the war, Professor Lowe built a narrow-gauge railway along the spine of the San Gabriel mountains above Pasadena to a peak which still bears his name. Lowe had come west in 1888 to build a gas plant, but was attracted by the scenic possibilities of the mountain range, towering above the city. The railway was part of a plan to have a chain of resort hotels built high in the mountains. The rickety cars of the train rattled along the narrow tracks dangerously skirting the edge of the sheer cliffs. For forty-five years the natives of the surrounding Los Angeles area as well as out-of-towners rode the professor's train, ate at his restaurant rest stops, and stayed at his hotels. A plan to construct a giant airship to carry passengers to the mountain peak failed to get off the ground. With his balloons, mountains, patents and investments, Professor Lowe left his mark in the history books and a lot of money for his granddaughter Florence to enjoy. Of this she did an excellent job!

* * *

3

The San Marino home was a place of genteel living where no one but the servants worked. The servants themselves were of a now-extinct class that enjoyed a close "part-of-the-family" relationship with their employers. They came when they were young and stayed for a lifetime. Neither Florence nor her mother knew how to cook but they knew their menus and proper table service. Each meal was served in a different room—there was a breakfast room, a luncheon room, and a very formal dining room. Butlers and maids scurried about, seeing to the family's slightest needs.

"Hell, I never heard the word *supper* except in some connection with the church," Florence once recalled.

Horses were a popular item around the Lowe estate and Florence's father saw to it that his daughter learned to ride properly at an early age. She was a competent rider of harness, five-gaited, reined, hackamore, jumping, and thoroughbred horses by the time she was five years old. She had been taught by experts such as Dr. Demming, Mouchel, and Dick Donley.

A young lady of the early 1900s had to be schooled in the social graces, so Florence's mother guided her through early classes in girl things. Among these was intense training in ballet and it was on the stage of Los Angeles Philharmonic Auditorium where Florence got her first taste of show business. She was a tiny child and a celebrated queen of ballet used her as a part of her performance. At the finale of her historic dance, she would lift the child ballerina, Florence, to her shoulders and together they would perform the final graceful pirouette to close the show. On a horse or on a stage, Florence was a gifted performer before she was six years old.

The next step in the programmed life of Florence Leontine Lowe was formal education which started at Los Angeles Polytechnic Elementary School where she was the only girl in a class of twenty-three boys. Among her classmates was Charles Paddock, the first man to run the 100-yard dash in less than 10 seconds. A short-lived stint at the Westridge School for Girls was next, but it was not a sufficiently disciplined school to contain the developing personality of

4

young Florence. She was next sent to the Ramona Convent in nearby Alhambra. After being schooled in the scholastic basics by the good sisters of the convent, Florence was sent to the posh Bishop Episcopal School for Girls in La Jolla, California. When she announced that she wanted to become a veterinarian, her mother quickly enrolled her in the Stickney School of Art.

At the end of her formal schooling, Florence felt that Zane Grey "was a damned good writer," and that *Lady Chatterly's Lover* was the most stupid and boring book that she had ever read.

Florence's mother, perhaps sensing the rebellious and adventuresome streak in her eighteen-year-old daughter, engineered a socially acceptable and proper marriage—to an Episcopalian minister, several years older than the young bride-to-be.

"My mother entrapped me by arranging early morning horseback rides with my husband-to-be. When we returned from the rides my mother hovered over us with tasty breakfasts. I'd graduated from the Bishop School at La Jolla where my future husband had made the baccalaureate speech and all of the girls had raved about him and how handsome he was. I was very religious at this time. I had spent several years in the Ramona Convent and as the Episcopal church was considered a society institution in Pasadena, my background made me an acceptable bride for the Reverend C. Rankin Barnes, the minister of that sacred, social edifice.

"I had a very beautiful and prestigious society wedding at which the men wore morning coats and striped pants. The church was banked with flowers and all of the Cadillacs and Lincolns in town were lined up for blocks around the church. After the wedding ceremony we went to the family mansion that had been moved brick by brick and stone by stone from Philadelphia, and had a reception and dance. The stag line lined up to kiss the bride and I, as bride, had quite an interesting time. I'd virtually never been kissed before. The funny little pecks my husband had given me were not anything like the kisses that these boys turned out. When

5

my husband's brother, Stanley N. Barnes, a future U.S. Attorney General, kissed me, I did a little serious wondering. The hot, flamboyant kisses made me realize that there might be a difference in men.

"My mother had provided a gorgeous and very expensive trousseau. Clothes pretty much bored me and the only real interest I had in them was for the tailored clothes for wearing in horse shows.

"Right after the reception I ran upstairs and put on the "going-away" part of my trousseau and the Reverend Barnes and I departed for our honeymoon suite at the Mission Inn in Riverside, California, where we had lovely rooms and a very big bed. My mother had arranged everything, right down to a gnat's eyebrow.

"I retired to the bathroom and put on a carefully fitted and beautiful nightgown. All of my life I had worn pajamas and I was very nervous in this uncomfortable garment. When I came out of the bathroom my husband looked at me from head to foot and then asked me to remove the nightgown. He had never seen a nude woman and was very curious. I refused to remove the gown and would not let him touch me. I suddenly realized that *I had ceased to be a human being and was instead an object of the curiosity of a man who had never before seen a naked woman.*

"I slept, or rather clung to a far edge of the bed until we arose early the next morning to catch a train for the Grand Canyon in Arizona. On the train we had separate berths.

"The canyon was beautiful and at sunset I remembered my mother's sense of humor, and of her delight in telling of how Douglas Fairbanks, Sr., originated the "Golly, what a gulley," when he first looked into the magnificence of the canyon.

"Dinner was excellent and I rather enjoyed wearing my new dinner dress. Immediately after dinner my husband steered me to our room. The room was away from the hotel with a slatted boardwalk leading to it. The night was gorgeous, the snow was deep, and the moisture of the snow had brought out the perfume of the pine trees. The room was rustic and had no bathroom. Romantic as hell with the right characters, but we sure didn't fit the part.

"My husband informed me that we had been married for four days and that he still didn't know anything about sex. He told me to take off my clothes and to get into bed because he was going to find out what sex was all about. I disrobed, got into bed, and lay stiff as a ramrod, embarrassed to the ears. He put my legs sort of up in the air and pulled them apart. I could feel him fumbling around like an inexperienced doctor with a blunt instrument. After a few moments of his fumbling I felt a sharp pain and the mental shock of the moment was worse than the physical. In another few moments he pushed my legs down and I looked into his face. He looked tortured, haggard, and miserable.

"I do not like sex. It makes me nervous. I see nothing to it. We shall have no more of it,' he said.

"I was relieved and happy to hear his announcement.

"The next day we rode mules down the Bright Angel Trail and spent the night in a shack in the canyon. The following day we rode the train back to our rectory home. There was no more sex nor was there a mention of it. Here I saw at a later date the parallel of my life with that of the beautiful Brett of Hemingway's *The Sun Also Rises*—except that I had no bullfighters waiting in the wings, nor in the bedroom."

* * *

Six weeks after her initial encounter with sex, Florence found that she was pregnant. A "virgin pregnancy" she called it. Everyone except Florence was happy about it. She was noncommittal and philosophically accepted it as being a part of the duties of a proper wife. Always do things properly had been her teachings.

She settled into the ways of the clergyman's wife, teaching Sunday School, entertaining visitors, embroidering veils for the chalice and doing it all with expertise. The new pattern was strange and cold and as her name had changed from Lowe to Barnes, her life had changed from happy to unhappy.

"More and more I realized that I was not cut out to be a minister's wife. I didn't know it at the time but it seemed that all of the women of the parish were in love with my husband. He liked it that way. He was getting an extreme lift from their adulation—whoops, almost said undulation! He would receive calls late at night and get me out of bed to go with him in his little car to strange houses. He never took me inside, always leaving me to wait in the car. His explanation was that some of the women he visited made advances toward him and he needed me for an escape excuse—his wife was waiting for him in the car! He was handsome, attractive, popular, and busy. I spent a lot of cold nights waiting in the little car and found the existence almost intolerable. More and more often I slipped away to my parents' home and spent time with my police dog, Nix, and my horses."

As the bundle within her grew and distorted her figure, Florence withdrew from all social and church activities. She continued to ride her horses and occupied her evenings with the making of highly embroidered baby clothes. When she went to the hospital for the delivery of her child she insisted that her dog Nix stay in the room with her. When the baby was born, Florence expressed more concern about the dog than about the new son.

"He was a large German police dog and he lived under my bed and I could trail my fingers over the side of the bed where he would touch them with his nose from time to time. He did not seem to object much to the baby which I breast fed. When I went home, the first thing I did was to put the baby on a blanket on the floor and let the dog 'nose' him over a bit. My mother had a fit. She was so afraid that the dog would harm the baby, but the very opposite happened and the police dog became the baby's protector. When either my mother or the nurse would approach the baby's crib, the dog would politely take their ankle with his mouth and would hold on until I told him to let go.

"With the baby, I was now reduced to keeping house and taking care of a small infant. I did not like the role a damn bit. My husband expected me to live on his salary of eighteen hundred dollars a year, plus the small free rectory house. This wasn't very much money and I'd been used to a helluva lot more. I was also used to servants in my father's house and I found the austere life of a minister's wife intolerable.''

To ease the family financial pinch and to put a little excitement in her life, Florence turned to nearby Hollywood—Tinseltown. She took care of animals that were used in the movies, rented her own trained dog and horses to the studios, worked as a script girl, and doubled for some screen stars. One of her first jobs was doubling for Louise Fazenda in the Rin Tin Tin pictures. She also did the horseback riding scenes in those Western movies where they used well-known sports figures for the heavies. One of the great heavyweights of the era was Sailor Jack Sharkey and Florence doubled for him in several movies.

The exposure to the Hollywood life style caused Florence to wonder anew about this sex business so she decided to give that subject a little study.

"Hollywood always talked a lot about sex and much of it went over my head. During the filming of a movie I met a young man named Gordon Pollack who was a cameraman for director Eric Von Stroheim. He was interested in me psychologically and wanted to see what made me tick. I suppose I was somewhat different from the other women he knew and he wanted to find out why. He sort of dissected me mentally and in the process used some strange words that I had to look up in the dictionary.

"After being around Hollywood for awhile and having learned a few things from Gordon, I propositioned my husband to have another try at it. We were standing on the stairway of our home, me a couple of stair steps below and he looking down on me. He became very upset with me, called me an animal, and the chasm between us widened."

Her mother died when she was twenty-one years old and Florence suffered a nervous breakdown.

"I inherited the money left by my grandfather and believing my father's story of community property, I signed half of the inheritance over to him. He promptly went out, remarried, and subsequently lost all of his money.

"I had a breakdown and the doctor said that it was caused by a heart condition and that I would not survive. I ran away and cured myself with exercise.

"I went all over the United States, always alone and did very little communicating with the people back home. I thoroughly enjoyed the freedom of travel, seeing new places and new things and learning a lot about my country.

"Eventually I arrived home in pretty good shape, my husband was reasonable about the whole thing, and didn't object too much to my running around with a bunch of young people I met after I got home.

"I had inherited a house at Laguna Beach so I ganged up with a bunch of Pomona College and U.S.C. people and we had some pretty wild parties there. Somewhere along about this time I got to know a young fellow named Marion Morrison who had a dog named Duke so people called him Duke. He later changed his name to John Wayne and did O.K. in movies.

"There was a lot of sex going on around the beach house and I suppose that everybody there except me was fucking somebody. All that sex activity really got me to wondering. I'd been married for four or five years and while everybody else, married or not, was having such a good time with sexual experiences, I wasn't doing anything. I decided that I was going to find out everything there was to know about sex, and was going to start at the beginning and dissect it leg by leg and wing by wing.

"I found a young man named Bill who had intrigued me. I found that he was sexually inexperienced and although I was the mother of a child, I knew nothing about sex. We ran around together for almost a year and other than a little heavy necking, we were just friends until we found that we had fallen in love with each other. A girl named Sylvia came along and started making passes at Bill but I hung onto him until we had to return for the fall semester at Pomona College.

"After he was back in school, Bill invited me to go with him to his fraternity cabin on Mt. Baldy where he was to replace some electrical wiring. It was to be an overnight trip and I enthusiastically agreed to go.

"The cabin was sort of rough with bunk beds along the walls and rustic furniture. The electrical work that was supposed to be the excuse for the trip was negligible but Bill tinkered with it long enough to make it appear as a legitimate reason for the trip.

"I had told Bill about my sexual experiences with my husband and of how horrible it had been. He knew that I was pretty skittish along these lines. As a student of horses and of horse language I told Bill that I had been sexually spooked.

"Bill started making love to me very slowly much as you would soothe a frightened colt. He started between my eyes and went all over my head. He caressed my neck, my shoulders, my body, my posterior, my legs, and the insides of my thighs much as you would treat a young colt not used to the touch of human hands. He slipped off my clothing slowly and carefully, talking quietly, kissing me from time to time and finally I stood in that rough cabin naked before a man. I was not embarrassed but felt very much at home. Bill removed his clothing very slowly and after he was naked we continued our activities in the cabin without a mention of sex. We stepped outside of the room and let the cool winds of the mountains kiss our naked bodies.

"He then carried me 'across the threshold' and put me on one of the bunks. He came into the bunk with me, fondled me gently, and told me how much he loved me. He kissed me everywhere, including the soles of my feet. His kisses were warm and open-mouthed and soon he had me hotter than a fox. When he entered me I hardly knew it because he held me very close and kept kissing me. He blew gently into my ear and tickled its inside with his tongue and before long we both became quite violent. I was enjoying the act as much as he was and I felt a great rise in my spirits. When it was all over we lay in the bunk, sweating and panting, quiet and happy. So this is fucking!

11

"It was a gorgeous night on the mountain. The moon was almost full and Old Baldy really shimmered under its autumnal glow. We showered together without embarrassment and went for a short walk. When we came back we did it again and it didn't take Bill long to warm me up because I was learning fast. We slept until late the next morning and during the drive back to Pasadena I couldn't keep my hands off of Bill. I wanted to do it over and over again. I wanted to make up for all the years that I had missed.

"When we reached the dry arroyo of the San Gabriel River I induced Bill to go for a walk and I seduced him while we were hidden by a giant boulder. The sands of the arroyo were very hot and the overhead noon sun was unforgiving as it blared down on our naked bodies. The heat of our passion shamed that of the sun and of the burning sands of the arroyo.

"When we arrived at my rectory home, I put Bill to bed in the guest room. I confronted the Reverend Barnes and told him exactly what I had done. It took a lot of retelling to convince him and once he believed it he broke down in tears. He told me to get Bill out of the house and that we were never to see him again. I agreed and took Bill back to his college. For awhile I kept my word, but I had tasted too deeply of the passion fruit and now craved it more than anything else in the world."

Florence returned to her horses but the physical strain of the separation from Bill proved too much for her and she began to deteriorate physically. Now the Reverend Barnes did a very strange and humane thing. As he was leaving for a convention in New Orleans, he suddenly jumped from the train, ran to the waiting Florence, embraced her, and said, "If you want that boy, you go get him," and then jumped back on the train as it was beginning to move out of the station.

Florence raced to Pomona College and when she told Bill the news, he quit school and returned with her to the rectory where they lived as man and wife. The nurse who was taking care of Florence's young son was so enraged with this unorthodox, "unchristian" arrangement that she moved out

12

of the house, taking the boy with her. Florence and Bill eventually retrieved the boy, and the nurse returned to live with them so that she would not be separated from the child. The nurse realized that Florence knew very little about her son, and even less about how to care for him.

"Of course I didn't have the slightest idea of what to do with the child. I had spent very little time with him, actually. However, he was still a little boy so Bill and I bought him lots of cap pistols, knives, the stuff you put in cap pistols to make them go "pop" and he had sort of a little camp in the house. We gave him a wild and glorious time and he had everything he wanted. I spoiled him terribly for a few days. At the end of the week, Nurse Ketchum came dragging back. She told me that she would keep her opinions to herself, would leave me alone, and that she couldn't stand to be separated from the child and to see the damage that I was doing to him."

The same day during which Bill had returned to live with Florence, a young Catholic priest came to visit her. He explained that a priest had to be very careful about his activities and knowing that the Reverend Barnes was off on convention business, it seemed the ideal circumstance for him and Florence to "have some fun." Florence called Bill who escorted the would-be errant priest from the house. This incident was one of the pieces that created the whole of Florence's later disagreements with organized Christianity as practiced by the dictates of a few human beings.

The *menage-a-trois* arrangement was a little sticky, so Florence put Bill up in a rental house she owned in South Pasadena far enough away to be discreet but close enough for her to run to for the sweet side of life. She and Bill both got jobs as electricians in the old movie studios called Poverty Row.

"I had a lot of fun running around the high parallels to adjust the lights for the scenes being filmed below.

"I continued to work with the horse operas whenever I could find jobs. My trained grey gelding, Platinum King, that I kept at a house I owned in San Gabriel, got better and better and I used to work him while sitting on Buster, my little black horse. Platinum King had a great sense of timing and he was the only horse I ever saw who could gallop up to a fast-moving stagecoach, allow a cowboy to leap from the coach to his back, and then race away from the coach.

"I carried heavy cameras, did doubles, worked as script girl, and even worked as a film cutter. I always loved the picture business because it was a matter of creation. In those days everyone entered into the spirit of creating something. Time and hard work meant nothing, only the picture. Each person working on the picture, no matter how small his task, felt that it was a part of his own life that he was putting into the picture.

"I also did a lot of riding in horse shows. One horse I rode was a dapple-grey gelding who belonged to the famous evangelist Aimee Semple McPherson. Aimee was quite a girl and she had appropriately named this horse Radiant. Aimee would come to the shows all dressed up in sidesaddle attire with a high silk hat and she would parade around and talk to people. She would ride Radiant out around the exercise ring and line-up with exhibition riders. I would dress in an outfit exactly like Aimee's and when we were in the entrance tunnel at the Ambassador Show Ring we would trade places. I took Radiant around that ring so fast and with my head hunched between my shoulders everyone thought it was Aimee who was riding. We changed places again in the tunnel and Aimee then took Radiant out to cool him down. Admirers gathered all around Aimee who happily took her bows. She paid me well to ride for her and I also enjoyed knowing her. Sometimes I would go to her Four Square Gospel Church and watch her put on her show. She never missed a bit, colored lights, angels, the whole show. I remember how she told her audiences not to desecrate the temple with the vulgar clinking of coins and to quietly put "folding" bills and checks into the collection plates.

"Aimee lived what you might call a double life. She was completely different when she was away from the church. As I remember her, she drank and smoked with the best of them. I recall an image of her standing with a cigarette and of smoke being blown out in great puffs through her wide flaring nostrils. She was very beautiful with lovely auburn hair heaped high on top of her head. Joe Flores, an excellent horseman, took care of Aimee's horse Radiant, and spent a lot of time with her. It was pretty well understood that when Aimee took her sabbaticals and did her disappearing act, that Joe went with her. I liked Aimee. She did everything with a flair and she had class.''

While Florence was doing her movie thing, riding in horse shows and making the overhead klieg lights work, she was still the legal wife of the Reverend Barnes and had to work at it sometimes.

''Every once in a while I had to go to some function with my clergyman husband. I went to weddings, funerals, and parties when he insisted. One of these events was a Pasadena society wedding and my dinner partner for the evening was Dr. Millikan of the California Institute of Technology. There had been a lot of publicity in the newspapers and magazines about Einstein and the atom and that Dr. Millikan was one of the few people who really understood the atomic theories of Einstein. I was horrified because I didn't know anything about an atom so what could I talk about with such an intellectual expert as Dr. Millikan?

''The party was gorgeous, a corsage of orchids for each lady guest, cocktails, excellent wines, and a superb dinner of filet mignon. Dr. Millikan and I tested each other for a suitable conversation. He tried women's clothes and found that I wasn't interested. I tried horses, he knew nothing about them. I took the advantage and laid it on a little about my extreme wealth of knowledge about horses. He retaliated by asking if I had studied Euclid in high school. I told him that I had flunked the course. This knowledge made him quite happy for he had written a textbook about Euclid. Score even, horses for me, Euclid for him. We were a perfect pair on the dance floor and others left the floor to watch us do our stuff. The dinner with Dr. Millikan that evening did a lot to help me get rid of a haunting inferiority complex for I discovered that no matter how much a person may know about any one subject, every other person has a subject that they know better than anyone else. So don't let someone else's knowledge get you down—there is bound to be something you know more about than anyone else."

In addition to her thirst for the gusto and excitement of life, Florence had a near insatiable appetite for knowledge. She read voraciously and her formal education was fortified by the liberal education she got through her reading and personal experiences.

One of Florence's favorite people and a firm friend was Will Durant. Whenever he was in the California area on one of his lecture tours, Florence volunteered to be his chauffeur. They were a strange pair, the gifted philosopher and the searching child of wealth but they shared a precious bond of friendship that transcended all differences.

Will Durant and Florence would visit the ships in Los Angeles harbor and spend hours in philosophic discussion. During one of these visits they made friends with Sataheechee Hartman, a Japanese poet who joined them in their inquiries into the ways of the world and of man. Hot saki was the fuel for the night when they would watch the new day break after having talked all through the night.

Whether it was the romance of the sea, the thirst for more knowledge, or the saki is not known, but for one reason or another Florence decided to go to sea. Not as a pampered cruise passenger, but as a crew member!

2

Florence Leontine Lowe Barnes, a socially prominent wife of an Episcopalian clergyman who knew absolutely nothing about ships nor their missions, conned her way aboard a rusty banana boat as an able-bodied seaman. Her first encounter aboard the boat was with a man named Roger Chute, the wireless operator. Chute, himself a free-spirit adventurer, worked his way around the ports of the world but he did not take kindly to the idea of a girl, disguised as a boy, doing the same thing. He was from the old school of superstition that believed that a woman aboard a ship was bad luck. Other than Chute's obvious dislike of her and his resentment of having her aboard, she was reasonably well-accepted by the rest of the crew.

The banana boat departed San Pedro harbor at dawn and after clearing the port, the crew took down the American flag from the mast and ran up their true colors of Panama. They also revealed that their cargo was guns and ammunition destined for some obscure group of Mexican revolutionists.

"These Mexican revolutionists were not paid troops or members of a paid army. They were Mexican-Indian farmers who did not own their land and it was not a revolution of major importance. When the sectionalized revolt erupted, the farmers were pressed into service to fight for some nebulous cause, the purpose and reason for which they did not know. At this time political relations between the United States and Mexico were somewhat strained and the revolutionary Mexican group hated and distrusted the gringos en masse.

"The battles of these revolutionaries ceased at sundown and some kind of an unofficial truce was declared. The 'soldiers' would eat, drink, tell ribald stories and sing far into the night. At daybreak, hangovers and all, the men dragged themselves to the battlefield to start their 'war' all over again."

Florence, hearing all of the hell raising that was going on at the beaches and being bored as hell on the boat, wanted to take a dinghy ashore to join in the fun. The sailors on the banana boat, knowing the dangers of both the bay and of the seaport village, refused to take her ashore.

The bay and the waters of this coast were popular fishing spots for commercial fishermen, both American and Mexican, and many ships illegally fished these waters. At that time there was a Mexican gunboat, *Tecate*, which patrolled these waters during the night searching for the unlicensed fishing boats. The illegal American boats, to avoid detection, would not anchor at night but would drift free in the bay—always ready for a fast escape. The bay was usually dotted with these free-floating, unlighted ships, and they were a constant menace to sea-lane navigation and a particular threat to a small hand-rowed dinghy. Small craft were always in danger of being run down by the outlaw ships.

Florence understood the threat to the safety of those who tried a night landing in a dinghy. But she let her desire for excitement override her judgment and insisted upon being rowed to the dock. Her stint in Hollywood, the parties at Laguna, and her association with the horse people had enriched her vocabulary far beyond that learned in the convent or finishing school. She could cuss as good or as bad as any sailor on the ship and she let it all out as she told them what a bunch of "fucking, lily-livered, lady-finger-eating, gutless bunch of sons of bitches" they all were. The sailors were impressed by her performance and even learned a few new words but they refused to pick up the gauntlet she had thrown down.

As she stood gazing longingly at the lights of the town, Florence was totally surprised when Roger Chute, her antagonist who didn't want her to be there in the first place, sidled up out of the darkness.

"C'mon, kiddo. Let's just take the dinghy and get out of here," he whispered.

The other crew members shrugged off their objections to the antics of Florence and Roger as typically "crazy gringo."

Rather than aim for the lights of the town, Roger and Florence chose the beach campfires of the soldiers. The voyage was a treacherous one and the occupants of the small boat questioned the wisdom of their adventurous decision. Like artful dodgers, they skirted the free-floating, unlighted fishing vessels that would suddenly loom from the darkness.

"It was damned scary. We both rowed furiously and a couple of times almost banged directly into the sides of the rolling ships. It was somewhat like the World War II troops must have experienced as they picked their way through floating mines. I was fucking well relieved when the campfires became more distinct and we could hear the rowdy singing of the Mexicans on the beach. The surf was pretty high and as we beached the dinghy we damned near let it dump us but we finally go it on the beach all in one piece."

Florence had signed on as a crew member under the assumed name of Jacob Crane and had adopted the clothing of a seafaring man. Her black hair was cut short, she wore a heavy man's work shirt a couple of sizes too large, grease-stained dungarees, and a pair of dirty sneakers. With a battered cap pulled low on her face, Florence looked more like a character from a Jackie Coogan movie than that of adventuress. But she passed easily as a male deckhand.

"You've got the temperament, language, and appearance to pass as a guy. I don't think we'll have any problems along that line," Roger observed.

Florence was more loquacious and colorful about her appearance.

"Any son of a bitch who thought I wasn't a guy was just asking to get knocked on his ass. One funny move and I'd set him on his ass so hard and fast that he'd wish that he'd kept his suspicions to himself."

19

They were well received by the drunken "revolutionaries" after they explained that they were from the ship that had brought them more guns and ammunition. After a night of raucous drinking and singing, the soldiers again went to do battle while Florence and Roger, she on a small gray burro and he on a large white horse, started their unauthorized visitor's trek across the wilds and wonders of Mexico.

* * *

The proper names given to children by their parents often seem terribly misfitted when the child becomes an adult and this was certainly the case with Florence Lowe Barnes.

"Come on now, can you imagine me ever being a Florence? That name implied everything that I wasn't. As a wife for the Reverend Barnes I suppose it was an O.K. name, but I never really was his wife anyway, so even that didn't fit. Old Roger changed all of that.

"One day as I watched him on the big white horse that the revolutionaries had given us, I thought about Don Quixote and how much he must have looked like Roger as he rode about the countryside of Spain tilting at windmills and rescuing beautiful ladies who were in distress. I told Roger about the resemblance and he looked down at me on my burro and told me that he agreed but that I looked a great deal like Quixote's servant-companion, Pancho. I chided him about his literary memory and corrected the servant's name to Sancho, as it was."

"Ah, what the hell, Pancho or Sancho, you fit the bill and from now on I'm calling you Pancho," Roger announced.

"With a built-in taste for showmanship I thought this was a great name. Pancho Barnes! Sort of a pleasant contradiction. I rolled the name around a little and it came out tasting sweet. Roger didn't know it, but he had christened me for life as Pancho Barnes, a name that fitted me physically and spiritually."

With her new identity as Pancho, Florence and Roger ultimately made their way to Mexico City where the entire town was engaged in celebrating Cinco de Mayo, one of Mexico's major holidays.

"The town was filled with drunken revelers. Huge bonfires threw a glow of orange on the walls of adobe buildings, casting grotesque shadows of drunken guerrillas who had executed several Mexican generals. The taste of blood was in the air and it was no place for Americans."

Finding that Germans were welcomed by the celebrating Mexicans, Pancho and Roger decided to be German so they could join in the wild parties in the cantinas.

"Instead of staying in our room as had been suggested by a waiter at dinner, we sallied forth to mingle in the activities of the celebrants. We were sitting at a table drinking beer when a drunken hulk of a soldier started paying us more than casual attention. He directed the attention of others toward us and we soon heard 'Americano' and 'Gringo' with alarming frequency and increasing disgust. We had to do something in a hurry to bolster our identity as German.

"Roger recited the opening line from *Watch on the Rhine* in German and I countered with a line from *Lorelei*. We then slapped each other on the back and laughed uproariously as if we had recited some juicy and obscene German joke. We repeated the act several times during the evening. There were no Germans there and none of the Mexicans understood German so we got away with the act and had a helluva good evening."

After Mexico City, Pancho and Roger literally hoofed it to Veracruz and here they got on a tramp ship *Tambalipas* and worked their way to Puerto Mexico, a small port on the Gulf of Mexico at the mouth of a river. Once aboard, they mingled with deck passengers and got to their destination without paying or working.

"The ship was packed with livestock, boxed cargo and passengers to where the deck was flush with the water. There were only a couple of cabins. We had no money so we fought the chickens, cows, pigs, and other passengers for space on the flooded deck."

Roger and Pancho had thumbed their respective noses at convention, Mexico, and the world and had emerged

21

unscathed but their luck suffered a change. Roger, who had scratched his legs on some coral while gathering shells, had neglected the scratches and allowed his legs to become seriously infected. Almost overnight, the scracthes turned into puss-filled ugly wounds with ominous red streaks running up his legs. Pancho recognized these symptoms of blood poisoning.

"I searched desperately for local doctors and finally discovered that an oil refinery a couple of miles inland had hospital facilities. There was no transportation available so I literally carried and dragged Roger the two miles. It was uphill through underbrush and tangled jungle-like vines. Roger was delirious with fever and was of little help during this awful trip."

The hospital accepted Roger as an emergency patient, lanced his legs, drained the poisonous puss and applied bandages. Roger and Pancho spent the night at the hospital and with the aid of crutches given to Roger by the hospital, they made their way back to the good ship *Tambalipas*. When they got back to the ship, they found everyone excited about the Dempsey-Tunney heavyweight championship fight. It was July 26, 1928.

Once back aboard ship, Pancho, still in her masquerade as a boy, was hired by a handsome young caballero to act as his bodyguard and to carry a cache of gold for him. Mexican currency was of little value and Mexicans with money carried gold pieces with them. This young man, Generoso Castro, soon posed a real problem for Pancho for her own femininity damn near betrayed her. She was strongly attracted to this dashing young Mexican man. But the spirit of adventure prevailed and she fulfilled her mission as "bodyguard" to the gold and left the romance for another day.

Pancho and Roger left the ship at Campeche and bummed across the Yucatan peninsula to Merida and on inland to visit the Yucatan ruins. Pancho carried a large bucket with her and each night she made Roger soak his still festering legs, drained the wounds, and dressed them in clean bandages.

After poking around all the ruins they could find, Pancho and Roger hoboed their way back to Merida. The brief exposure to the ancient history of Mexico infected Pancho with an interest that lasted for a lifetime.

The only room available for the money that they had was the temporarily absent "Number One" girl's in the local whorehouse. This bit of risque living delighted Pancho and she lived, high, wide, and handsome in these gaudy surroundings until the queen of the whorehouse returned and flew into a fiery Mexican rampage. Pancho and Roger were kicked out with a flourish and the indignant lady resumed her throne.

"Being kicked out of a Mexican whorehouse sort of dents the dignity. But under the circumstances I didn't have time to fight with those stupid assholes."

Roger was still having trouble with his legs. They were out of money and it was time to go home, so they went to the American consul for help. He made arrangements for these "young men" to work their way home as able-bodied seamen on a clunker named *Rajah*. They were assigned quartermaster duties and had an uneventful voyage to New Orleans—except for one small incident.

"Imagine my surprise when I found that my ever-lovin' Generoso Castro was on the same ship. Circumstances were different this time but the less said about that the better. By the time we got to New Orleans he damn well knew that I wasn't an able-bodied seaman. Able-bodied for sure but no way a man."

Once in New Orleans they headed for a dockside restaurant and a change of diet from the tortillas and frijoles of the past few months.

"I had a passion for frogs legs and when I asked this tough waitress if she had frog legs she hiked up her skirt, showed some shapley legs, and asked whether I thought they looked like frog legs. Well, I didn't get frogs legs, but we got along good with this waitress and wound up with a helluva good creole dinner."

Pancho and Roger hitchhiked, conned rides on buses and trains, lived in hobo jungles, and ate whatever they could find. They were arrested in Austin, Texas as vagrants, given twenty-five cents each for a flop house bunk, and told to get out of town. They did, early the next morning.

"Once we got to San Diego, I called the house in Pasadena and they either came after us or sent money, I don't remember which. After all, having gone all over Mexico on foot and without funds, getting from San Diego to Pasadena is hardly worth remembering."

A trapped social butterfly named Florence Leontine Lowe Barnes had left the Pasadena mansion. A physically hardened adventuress named Pancho had returned.

3

After Pancho returned to the San Marino house and the routine of normal living, she was restless and got bored very easily. Even her horses, forays into Hollywood, and the parties at the Laguna Beach house didn't satisfy the restlessness within her. She had had a good go at the life of adventure and had developed an appetite for the unusual. She was searching. A cousin opened an avenue toward a new and exciting experience when he invited her to go with him to the airfield where he was taking flying lessons.

"We went out to the flying field in Arcadia near where Santa Anita race track is now. It was a very small field having been originally planned as a balloon field. There were two immense balloon hangars and a mooring mast on the field. A man named Ben Catlin had two airplanes on the field. Fairchild Aerial Mapping Concern had a couple of old DH-4 airplanes, Western Air Express came in from time to time, and several other pilots kept their airplanes on the field. My cousin, Dean Banks, introduced me to Mr. Catlin and told him that I would like to learn to fly. After I told him that I wanted to start right away, he stuck a helmet and goggles on me, strapped me in the back seat of an old airplane, and we took off.

"We flew around for awhile, did a few mild maneuvers, and landed. We agreed on another flight the following day and what a flight that was! He did everything that could be done with an airplane: stalls, loops, spins, rolls—the works. I thought that these violent yet graceful actions were a normal part of flying; I was too stupid to know that I'd been 'wrung out.' "

After the landing Ben asked Pancho, "Still want to learn how to fly?"

"Hell yes I want to learn to fly. That's what I'm out here for," she answered.

"O.K.," said Ben Catlin, "I've had thirty-three women students so far and not a one of them has soloed. I've been getting a little discouraged but if you want to learn I suppose I'll have to try to teach you."

"The next day Ben started teaching me the airplane and how to manipulate stick and rudder and how to use hand signals. We had no parachutes because Ben couldn't afford them. There was no communication system between the two open cockpits in the plane, not even the simple Gossport funnel and tube system; it was all done with hand signals.

"When Ben motioned down with his hands, it was to put the nose down, or up for nose up. When he put his hand out to one side, that meant to pick that wing up or when he placed his hand on his right cheek, it was to tell me that I was slipping or skidding to the right and vice versa for the left. Ben had a simple, easy and comfortable way of instruction. Many years later I tried to be as good an instructor as Ben had been because with good solid signals and understanding a student is always aware of what's going on. Ben taught me to fly straight and level by following the roads. Then we went to turns and on to the figure-eight. After I could perform all of the aerial maneuvers to Ben's satisfaction, he started on landings. The field was very small and there always seemed to be a prevailing crosswind. The approach to the field was lined with tall eucalyptus trees and some of them had been cut down to make an airplane pathway through them. They weren't too damn generous with the clearance they provided, for a large airplane's wingtips barely cleared the trees.

"I learned to side-slip through this pathway, straighten out the airplane, and pop it onto the ground without so much as a skip. The landings always looked spectacular but they were just sweet and simple normal procedure.

"Most of my student flying was in an OX-5* Travelaire owned by a fellow named Jimmy Robeson and rented to Ben. The other ship was a Waco OX-5 that Ben also rented. The OX-5 was a Curtis WWI Engine of 90 HP and only a single magneto.

"After I became proficient in the basics of flying, Ben taught me aerobatics. We did wingovers, loops, rolls and spins. I enjoyed these maneuvers very much and was always relaxed while we were doing them. Matter of fact, I got too damned relaxed sometimes.

"One day after a fifteen-minute lesson, Ben kicked the Travelaire into a spin at about 1200 feet, spun down to about 50 feet above the ground, pulled out, went around the pattern and landed. He crawled out of the airplane and leaned against the fuselage and I joined him.

"You were pretty low on that last spin, Ben, but I'm getting so used to these maneuvers that I never get scared anymore," I told him.

Instructor Ben Catlin rolled his eyes heavenward and turned away from Pancho so she wouldn't notice the deep green of his face. The rudder had stuck in an extreme position and Ben had fought it all during the spin, finally breaking it loose at the last moment. He stopped doing low-level dare-devil spins after that.

Shortly after this incident, Jimmy Robeson, the owner of the ship, was killed when he failed to recover from a spin. Pancho did not witness the accident but shortly thereafter she did see a spectacular accident that gave her a closer look at the more sober side of flying.

"Joe Brown was a pro, a high-flying government pilot and when Jim Grainger, an airplane dealer, brought a new OX-5 Swallow over from Clover Field (Santa Monica) for us to fly, Joe volunteered to fly it.

"The Swallow was a floater, not at all like the Jennies that came down like streamlined bricks. If you really didn't fly right down to the spot where you wanted to land, the

---

*OX-5 was a magnificent v-shaped engine that powered many of the early airplanes.

27

Swallow would float right on by it. After Joe flew the Swallow around for awhile he floated right by the landing strip and repeated this performance during two subsequent landing attempts. On his third attempt we were all out on the field jumping up and down and giving Joe the signal to land. We got poor old Joe so excited that he ran into the mooring mast in the center of the field and the airplane bounced over onto the Pacific Electric Railroad which at that time ran right through the area that is now Santa Anita racetrack. The old poles that supported the wires for the trolley cars were like matchsticks and when Joe hit them there was a sheet of flame that shot high in the air and he sheared twenty-eight of the poles. No one believes that he knocked down twenty-eight poles but I know damned well that it's the truth because I counted them—personally.

"I jumped in my car and by driving down the tracks was the first one to reach the accident. Joe was out of the airplane leaning against a post. He was bruised and bloody but basically O.K. Although we knew that the broken poles and disrupted electric wires would keep any street cars from running any time soon, Ben wanted to get the airplane off of the streetcar right of way. Ben yelled for me to go to the hangar and get the tail dolly because airplanes didn't have tail wheels in those days and a wheel dolly was put underneath the tail to move them about. When I got to the hangar I found that the DH airplane was on the dolly and there was no one there to help me move it. It was estimated that the DH tail put about 750 pounds of pressure on the tail dolly and it normally took three men to move it off and on the dolly.

"By putting my back under the aft fuselage of the DH I raised it off the dolly, kicked the dolly free, and lowered the tail to the floor. It was one of those phenomena that interested me for the rest of my life. I towed the dolly to the accident scene and when I got there Ben asked how I got the dolly from under the DH. I told him and although everyone knew that the DH was on the dolly, no one believed my story. It is one of those stories in aviation that's told about me and which no one ever believes. Later in life, when I recalled this incident and other strange things that I had done, I realized that I am sometimes under a state of self-hypnosis that allows me to do things that are normally impossible and usually denied me.

"We finally got the wrecked airplane back in the hangar and Joe Brown took off on a drunk to chase girls and show what a man he was even after flirting with the death head. That night about midnight Joe showed up at my place and asked if he could sleep with me. All that he wanted was sympathy and company so I told him O.K. He'd already laid his girl friend and another girl he had picked up to prove what a man he was and how he could take it. Right after a death-defying spectacular crash he could still run around screwing the girls all night. When he got to my place, it was all out of his system and he wanted someone close to assure him that everything was really O.K."

Pancho's happy band of aerial bandits was kicked off of Arcadia field after Joe Brown's spectacular accident. The government officials professed to knowing nothing about these renegades operating from the military field. All of the Arcadia aircraft were moved to the field at Culver City.

Claude Ryan who built Lindbergh's *Spirit of St. Louis* had imported a Seaman-Holsky engine from Germany and installed it in a Travelaire aircraft. Shortly before moving from Arcadia to Culver City Pancho bought one of them. It was an ironic sort of ownership for although she owned the airplane no one would give her an approved check-out so that she could solo the airplane. This problem she solved the hard way.

"After we were run off from Arcadia, Ben kept his house there and I continued living in the big house in San Marino. Ben was distressed about losing his flying school and it seemed that nothing would convince him to move with us to the new field at Baldwin Park. We would go over to Ben's and drop a few bucks to him in poker games but that didn't help much either. Finally, he gave in and continued his school at the new field.

"Now I had a unique situation. I owned my own airplane, I knew how to fly, but no one would let me solo my own damned airplane. A friend of my cousin Dean's named Dale Straw claimed to be a competent pilot who had soloed Jennies. So the three of us literally stole my own airplane. With Dean and me as passengers and Dale at the controls we took off for San Diego. Dale had such a tough time getting the airplane on the ground at Ryan Field in San Diego that I wondered if he had ever flown at all. I was so mad at Dale after he fucked up the landing that I was determined to fly it myself. One of Claude Ryan's pilots named Red Harrington took me for a check flight and then refused to approve me for solo. So it was back to home base with Dale again at the controls.

"Before giving up on the solo, we landed at Santa Ana where Johnny Martin gave me a ride and he too refused to let me solo so we really gave up."

While Pancho and her two playmates were tooling around looking for a benevolent instructor who would approve her solo flight, the day grew late, cloudy, and foggy.

"It got very foggy and we were so low we were just skimming the ground. It was getting foggier, the sun was going down, and we were like babes in the woods sitting up there in that airplane. Neither Dean nor I could land it. Dale wasn't doing too well at it and the weather was getting worse. Our flying ability and the weather both equaled to a big fat zero.

"A big open field showed up beneath us and Dale cut the throttle and we just sort of plopped on the field. We found that it was Compton. We left the airplane there and went home. I went back and took some lessons from Leo Root but he was never satisfied that I was ready to solo. Ben was so pissed-off at Dean and me for our San Diego flight that he kicked us out of his new school and refused to bring the airplane from Compton. He would not allow us to fly with anyone on his new field."

Pancho, Dean, and Dale tried all of their old con games on Ben and it was only after they gave him the cold shoulder treatment that he accepted them back in his flying school in Baldwin Park. The field there was in a dry river bottom with a deep sand base and power lines at one end of the field. For some obscure reason it seemed that every small airport had to have some obstruction over one end or the other. The hangar was a small inconsequential one and there was a hot dog and pop stand where everyone hung out. Among some of the airport bums were Nelse Griffith, Al Blakely, Wayne Merrill, and John Nagel. It was here where Pancho got serious about her flying and where Ben Catlin finally let her solo.

"One day after about six hours of actual in-flight instruction in my airplane Ben decided to let me solo. He promised to solo me if I could make six consecutive perfect landings. After many attempts I got six in a row and Ben climbed out, leaving me to solo. This was one of the highlights of my life. I poured on the power, roared down the field, and literally jumped the plane into the air. I think that the first thing a student notices on a solo ride is the absence of the instructor. Me, I was so glad to get rid of him, I hardly noticed. Without him, the airplane took off much easier. I climbed, circled around for awhile, and brought the ship in for a perfect three-point landing. I had soloed! I was a pilot! Nobody could tell me anything from then on! In those times I had joined a rather select group. No matter what else I was, I was a pilot."

It is often said that you can always tell a pilot—but not very much! After all of the care of getting ready to solo and the well-executed solo flight, Pancho carried her first passenger—after only five or ten minutes of solo time.

"My friend, Nelse Griffith, was my first passenger and we put on quite a show. After a few minutes of boring and routine flying, Nelse stepped out onto the wing and held on to the flying wires. I came down low across the electric wires at one end of the field and made a high-speed pass across the field. We did all sorts of aerobatics and hedge-hopping with Nelse hanging on the wires. We put on a real show and by the time we landed I had started carving my own niche in the world of aviation."

Pancho and her cousin Dean Banks developed a little air war of their own, each continually striving to beat the other's aerial achievements. Whenever one would get a new airplane, the other would immediately try to get one that was faster and more maneuverable. They spent a lot of money in this competition and as the quality of their airplanes grew, so did their capabilities and their appetites for adventure.

"We were like a lot of young birds that just got their wings and found out how to use them. We were out flying all day, trying out various things, feeling out the air, feeling what we could do with it, and each evening we gathered for a hangar flying session.

"Our hangar flying wasn't a social get-together but was deadly serious discussion. There were a great many things that people did not understand about airplanes. The airplanes were very unstable. We joked about all airplanes having inherent instability and of Jesus Christ always riding a wing-tip. It was the lessons learned during these hangar discussions that kept many of us alive.

"We used to fly around until we found a good flat-top cloud and then practiced landings on it. When we missed, stalled and went into a spin, we had theoretically killed ourselves. For some air shows we used to pick a nice cloud that was about a thousand feet above the ground on the bottom and come spinning out of it very spectacularly.

"Another glorious thing that happened to us was that about fifty little airports within a few miles of Los Angeles suddenly developed. We had lots of new pilots and lots of company. Many people started flying because of the impetus that Lindbergh had given the flying world with his flight across the Atlantic Ocean in 1927. Lots of new aircraft were being produced. We hopped from airport to airport, met old friends and new pilots. We had hangar parties at various fields and in our homes, and we talked mostly of airplanes and flying. We showed off for each other and for air show audiences. We were damned good. We dressed dramatically for the part and were always a source of interest. We swaggered a bit in our helmets, goggles, white scarf and boots. It was truly the golden age of flying and we were the cast."

The free-wheeling "wild blue yonder" romance of flying was caught up in the bureaucratic processes about this time and the U.S. Department of Commerce became the ruling authority. The authorities chased renegade pilots all across the country in an effort to control the fast growing aviation community. Pilots were taken to task about their flying credentials on a catch-as-catch-can basis. Pancho, finally caught in the web of aviation organization, relented and submitted to the rigors of a flight check. She was checked out by a Mr. Hollenbeck at the American Airport on Western Avenue and was awarded her license. Now she was not only a pilot but a pilot with credentials!

4

"Before I ever had a license I used to fly down to Ensenada and Tijuana in Mexico to visit with the rumrunners who assembled there. We used to go down there on their pay days and pick up a hundred bucks or so flying these guys around at ten bucks a hop. I used to stack these rumrummers in the airplane and take anyone else along who had the price. One time I had seven people in the old Ryan airplane—a Mexican man, his pregnant wife and their four kids. Don't know whether it's fair counting the unborn one, but it tends to make a better story.

"Border crossing was no problem because no one was used to having airplanes running around all over the world and the Mexican people and I were always close friends anyway.

"We used to rattle our ships up and down the local streets barely missing the buildings. There were a couple of little airports that were almost side by side and some pilots used to duck into them and put up a sign advertising stunt rides for five dollars per passenger. One of these pilots chose the wrong time to put on a real show and put his airplane through all of its paces about 500 feet above the field. Jimmy Hall, a flight inspector, was at the other field and when the stunt pilot landed, Hall rushed over and fined him $500 for violating regulations and doing stunts with passengers aboard. The next day the stunt pilot had a new sign as his airplane advertising stunt rides for *$505* a flight!"

The flying fraternity was, and still is, to some degree, a close knit group of mutual admirers. The shared fun and heartbreaks of flying tended to weld the participants into some common way of understanding. Humor was a special thing and was best understood by those in the inner circles of flying. Acts such as wing walking and parachuting which appeared to be great risks and the product of intense courage were to the pilots only every day's routine happenings. Pancho always sensed and recognized the thunder.

"At the field in Baldwin Park we became more active—more people, more airplanes, more flying, and more social activities. The camaraderie and friendships of this group can never be equalled in any other common pursuit. It was during one of these informal hangar get-togethers where I met a great big tall broad-shouldered boy named Slim Zaunmiller. He was six foot two, raw-boned and heavy. He loved parachute jumping. Slim had a chute that was fitted into a bag that was tied to the wing of the airplane and to a home-made harness which he wore. When he jumped out of the airplane, the chute spilled out of the bag and Slim then made a perfect parachute descent. It always gave everyone a thrill for it looked for a moment as though Slim had jumped out of the plane without a parachute. I'd usually drop him from about a thousand feet and Slim was so good that he could land right in front of the crowd. We passed the hat among the spectators to pay Slim for his jumping performances.

"When things were slow, Slim would flirt with a girl until he had her all pepped up about him. He had a way with the girls because in those days there was something heroic and romantic about a parachute jumper and Slim played that advantage to the hilt. He would get a girl interested in him and talk her into going for a ride in the airplane. With the girl in the front cockpit, Slim would pour the romantic coal on and get her into the parachute harness. After he got her safely in the harness, I'd pull up and over and while upside down dump her out of the airplane. I had developed a special technique for these girl jumpers where I'd kick the tail of the plane around so that they would always clear it. The girls always landed safely and without injury and we would try to land and be the first one to her. Slim would smooch her a bit and pat her on the fanny and she would be ready to make a jump of her own. The crowd always paid more to see the girls jump. Pull a trick like that today and you'd be sued by everybody including the Supreme Court."

Up until a few years ago, all student pilots had to demonstrate their ability to recover an airplane from a spin. A safe altitude of six to seven thousand feet was selected and the plane was then "kicked" into a spin by allowing it to stall and then putting in enough rudder and aileron to cause the plane to start a nose-down corkscrew descent. Most airplanes want to fly straight and level so the best spin recovery is to just relax on the controls and let the airplane recover. Because the airplane may not be one of those that "wants" to recover or because there may not be sufficient altitude for a natural recovery, there were "spin recovery procedures." "Way back when" it was a pilot's fear that those spins requiring 4000 feet for recovery usually started at 3000 feet!

Pancho and Ben had a rather unpleasant experience with spins when she first started flying and both of them sort of shied away from them whenever they could. It was inevitable, however, that the bureaucratic licensing procedures would force their hands and put them back in spinning airplanes.

"Ben was not making it financially at Baldwin Park so he took a job running an airport at Carpenteria, California for a very wealthy man named Jack Chadbourne who decided he wanted to be in the flying business. When Ben left Baldwin Park it almost broke up the old gang and even the little hamburger stand closed. We used to have a delightful time at the hamburger stand eating cannibal sandwiches which consisted of raw meat, onion, and mayonnaise or mustard between a couple slices of bread.* Ben said that he was of a

---

*This became a lifetime appetite for Pancho and I have been with her many times when she made this concoction in public and ate it with gusto.

peculiar nature that required raw meat so we copied that as we did most of the things which Ben did.

"I used to fly from Baldwin Park to Carpenteria most every day because I wanted to be around Ben and there wasn't anything else to do anyway. Jack Chadbourne, the owner of the field had an old Fairchild with a J-5 engine and wings that folded which we all called the "Old Homestead." He also had several other ships. Ben did a lot of charter work and flight instruction for Jack.

"It was at Carpenteria where I first met Al Larry, a wild pilot who grew even wilder as time passed. Al and I took our commercial flying tests on the same day. He took his test in a Jenny and I took mine in my Travelaire. I had to demonstrate spins to the inspector and Ben was so leery of spins that he would not go with me to practice. Ben gave me some ground instructions, found an old parachute for me to wear, and sent me into the wild blue to do some spins.

"On the first attempts I could not make the airplane spin so I landed and had lunch with Ben. I was afraid to spin the damned airplane! Ben admitted that he, too, was afraid of spinning that airplane but he wasn't taking a flying test so the problem was all mine. I took off again but could not muster the courage to sit and let the airplane fall off into some gruesome spinning maneuver so I kicked it into a violent spin entry. It was a spectacular spin, the recovery was great, and I passed the test."

*　*　*

Night flying in the late twenties was not too popular because there were few lighted runways and fewer night navigation aids. Pancho started staying later and later at Carpenteria and often arrived back at Baldwin Park after dark. She would often have to circle Baldwin Park until a passing car's headlights would illuminate the side of the old deserted hamburger stand. Using this as an immediate reference, she would line up with the riverbed and make her landing. To lose altitude rather quickly during an approach that was lined or restricted by an obstacle, pilots often used a maneuver called a side-slip. This was done by "cross-controlling" or more simply by using the ailerons (roll control surfaces) for a turn in one direction and the rudder (directional control) for a turn in the opposite direction. This caused the airplane to fly somewhat sideways or in a "side-slip" where the nose of the airplane was pointed several degrees from the actual path of the airplane. The maneuver looks similar to an automobile whose frame has been bent out of line. The car is actually going straight but the body is aimed crookedly. A side-slip is particularly dangerous in some airplanes because too much of aileron or rudder could cause the airplane to "snap-roll" and go into a spin. When used during low approaches it is particularly dangerous because there is not sufficient altitude in which to recover from spins. Many cadets met untimely deaths in some of the training airplanes when they found themselves too high on the final approach or not properly aligned and would try to "cheat" a bit by using the side-slip. Their lack of skill would allow them to put in a bit too much rudder to increase the angle of side-slip, the airplane would snap-roll, and they would hit the ground. Good instructors would always take their students to altitudes of eight to ten thousand feet to demonstrate the dangers of this cross-control procedure. As the student "slipped" the airplane, the instructor would tap in a bit more rudder, the airplane would snap and enter a spin. The altitude was sufficient for safe recovery and the student would be well aware of the dangers of side-slipping.

It was this side-slip maneuver that Pancho used to clear the high wires at the end of the Baldwin Park airport.

"As the return flights home became later and later, I was soon making the return trips in total darkness. After spotting the field I would side-slip the Travelaire over the eucalyptus trees and high wires and plop it down on the sandy field. I soon got so good at night flying that I was taking passengers over the city to see the night lights of Los Angeles. In those days there were lots of dark spots in the Los Angeles Basin and now on a clear night the whole basin looks like a single sheet of flame.

"Flying sure put me in touch with a lot of people and they were usually very interesting types. Little romances along the way always helped me to make life more fun. Jack Chadworth, who was Ben's boss, took quite a fancy to me. When we were together he used to sing "I Can't Give You Anything But Love, Baby" when in reality he could have given me a million dollars just as easy as love. I never did feel particularly romantic about Jack, but he was always very elegant in his actions toward me. One night he got drunk and gave me his hopped-up racing car as a gift. It would do 140 miles an hour. When he sobered up, I gave the car back to him but he'd get drunk and we'd repeat the whole act over again. This routine went on for a long time.

Andy Smith was another great flying buddy. He was the Army Air Corps Flight surgeon at March Field in Riverside, California and one helluva good pilot. He was an old crony of Ben's and I met him during one of his visits to Carpenteria. I never cared much for liquor but I always felt that I should be a good scout and drink with the rest of them. Big, bluff, rough Andy Smith used to love to pour a few drinks down me and then make me take a sobriety test before I would fly from Carpenteria back to Baldwin Park. He would make me stand on one foot with my eyes closed and arms stretched out in front while I slowly counted to fifteen. If I could do this act, he would give an O.K. to go fly. I got so expert at this test that I could do it perfectly although I was too drunk to walk. As I said, I didn't like to drink but always felt that it was my patriotic duty to defy the prohibition laws of the government in the best traditional manner.

"It was also at Carpenteria where I met Bob Short, a very gorgeous-looking and downright handsome exponent of the male sex. He was over six feet tall, regular features, dark hair, deep-brown eyes, broad shoulders, and a waist that tapered to slim hips. He was pleasant to talk with but he had a very mean streak and was such a lawless flier that the Air Corps had thrown him out. He had a very bad reputation and it was hard for him to get jobs. He asked me for a ride from Carpenteria and after a couple of good looks at that handsome face and strong body I agreed to take him with me. The flight was at night and after the landing, Bob helped me to hangar the airplane and, driving my car, headed for my house in San Gabriel. Bob was one of those fellows who never took time for a build-up and I was quite impetuous because we both aroused the worst in each other. As soon as we hit the house, we started on a real rough-and-tumble, all-out, sex affair. I had a big comfortable canopied bed and after the luxury of that setting we made violent and raptured love all over the house. There was a big white bearskin rug in front of the fireplace in the library and it always appealed to me as an especially sensitive spot for making love. Bob and I acted out all of our sex fantasies on that rug. I think that I got the idea from a movie called *The Merry Widow* with Mae Murray and made by Eric Von Stroheim where she is lounging very voluptuously on a white bearskin rug with black-lace scanties on.

"Bob and I found it quite interesting to romance each other on top of a nine-foot grand piano and under the library table. I don't know what the hell was the intrigue of making love in these strange places when we had such a luxurious bed. Guess that we figured that beds were just made for sleeping.

"Bob Short stayed around my place for a long time for he was really worth keeping. Things went along fine until he stole my airplane one day and I kicked him out. About this time the Chinese and the Japanese were having some kind of war and Bob got a job ferrying airplanes to the Chinese. The airplanes Bob was ferrying were loaded with ammunition and were ready for combat. During one of his ferry missions Bob was attacked by three Japanese fighters and although he shot down all three of his attackers in the action he was shot down and killed. Bob had lived a short and violent life and he died a violent death. He was a damned good pilot although he was thrown out of the Air Corps. Goddamned Air Corps never could recognize real talent. The Chinese erected a big monument to Bob and made him some kind of a national hero. It's a funny thing how some people can be complete sons of bitches and wind up as some kind of a fucking hero."

5

A "forced" landing, the name of which has now given way to an "emergency" or sometimes "precautionary" landing is one where the pilot is "forced" to land the plane because of some major malfunction or failure. Usually there is little time for planning the landing or for selecting a landing site. In the case of a single engine airplane, the failure of the engine is the most common cause for "forced" landings.

During training and subsequent "check rides" with inspectors, pilots are required to demonstrate their skill at making the "forced" landing. The instructor retards engine power to idle and informs the student that he has simulated a failed engine. The student must then put the airplane in the proper attitude, select the spot for the landing, and fly an approach to the spot. After it becomes obvious that he could or could not have successfully landed the plane, engine power is advanced and the flight continues.

Pancho experienced many real "forced" landings and became very proficient at landing on roads, plowed fields, golf courses, etc. She had no patience with latter-day flying inspectors who would simulate engine failure and make her demonstrate the forced landing technique. During one such check flight from Edwards Air Force Base to Oxnard, California, a flight over mountains, the check pilot pulled back engine power and told her to show him her forced landing technique.

"Bullshit. I've made so many forced landings I can do them with my eyes shut. Knock off this juvenile stuff and let's get on to Oxnard," Pancho argued.

"Nope," the instructor insisted, "You have to demonstrate."

"O.K., you asshole, here we go," Pancho yelled, and she killed the engine.

"Simulated, Pancho, not for real. Start that engine, we're in the mountains," the instructor pleaded.

"Screw you, forced you wanted and forced you'll get," Pancho replied.

Very gently she stalled the airplane into the tops of some scrub trees on a slight incline. The slow-moving airplane grated to a stop with its fabric shredded by the tree branches. The inspector was faint but he survived. Pancho was unhurt and hilarious. It took a special truck and a bunch of mechanics to disassemble the airplane and get it to an airport. Pancho "busted" her check ride but had a lot of fun doing it. Back in the "golden days" forced landings were "fun."

"I don't know why I've never mentioned forced landings. I've had quite a few but never paid much attention to them when we were still in the OX-5 stage. I used to fly a lot of OX-5 Jennies because I found them interesting and fun to fly. The OX-5 engines had two things that would go wrong with them. One was magneto failure and the other was that the carburetor float valve would stick. Either of these failures would put you in somebody's backyard or plowed field and it was fortunate that we had lots of open area to choose forced landing sites. Another advantage was that the aircraft were not very fast and most of us were used to short field landings anyway.

"My Ryan started developing engine trouble and on one trip to San Francisco in just a couple of days I had eight forced landings. After the landings I used to clean up the engine myself, freeing up the stuck valves and cleaning the fouled spark plugs. I had the damned thing in and out of shops and no one seemed to be able to fix it. One night, coming in from San Francisco to Carpenteria, it started backfiring so badly that it lighted up the black sky like a Chinese New Year. It scared the hell out of me. I decided that if no one could fix it that I would get rid of it. I landed at

Clover Field in Santa Monica and told a dealer there that I wanted to trade for a new airplane. He traded me the sweetest ship that ever lived—a speedwing Travelaire with a J-5 engine. It was unfortunate that the poor boys who bought my old ship crashed it during a forced landing, killing one and crippling the other one for life. It was a shame that it had to happen that way. They were nice guys.

"My cousin Dean Banks and I had a long-standing feud going about who had the fastest airplane and when I got my new Speedwing, Dean really had something to worry about. I now had a ship with which I could really outrun him. His Warner Scarab Travelaire couldn't begin to keep up with me. Dean then bought a $25,000 Travelaire cabin job and I had to streamline and polish my Speedwing to stay in the race with him. Why we all raced each other I'll never know but it seemed important at the time.

"On February 22, 1929, the Glendale, California airport was opened. My airplane was at Metropolitan Airport but I did a lot of flying in and out of Glendale. During this time I was also becoming acquainted with all of the motion picture and stunt pilots of the world. The most talented and colorful of them all was Frank Clark and he became a vital part of the most important part of my life in aviation.

"Frank could fly my Speedwing and really make it talk. It was a light airplane and was originally built for an OX-5 but I had a J-5 in mine. Frank would dive it at a landing field at about 200 miles an hour, get close to where he had to clear the wires that were always around airports, kick it to where it went broadside, and drop it in over the wires. In some ways I was afraid to fly with Frank because he was a diabolical soul in many respects."

During one of the early promotional flights from Glendale, Pancho raced the flamboyant Roscoe Turner from San Francisco to Glendale. Roscoe was the epitome of the romantic Knight of the Sky with his waxed mustache, gabardine riding breeches, soft suede jacket, helmet and goggles, white silk scarf and high polished boots. He carried a pet lion named Gilmore with him for an added touch of adventure. Pancho had secretly had her airplane hopped-up for added speed and she knew that she could beat Turner. But she wanted to do it with a flair.

She learned of a football game that was to be played in San Francisco at about the time the race was to begin so she carried an aerial movie camera with her in the airplane. She arranged to have a processing technician waiting to meet her after the race-ending landing. The technician was to ride a motorcycle and to meet Pancho as she rolled to a stop.

After she and Roscoe took off from San Francisco, Pancho flew over the football stadium and photographed several of the plays. She then headed for Glendale and landed there several minutes ahead of Roscoe. She handed her movie camera to the waiting technician. He sped away on his motorcycle and Pancho posed for the newsreels. At the victory banquet that night Roscoe was a somewhat graceful loser until Pancho announced that she would have landed earlier except that she had lingered en route to watch a football game. The doubting crowd laughed politely. Pancho had the lights turned down and her technician showed the hurriedly-processed film that Pancho had taken.

"I would have stayed to watch the whole game and still got here ahead of Roscoe but it was rather boring."

Roscoe Turner wasn't bored! He was furious with an anger which lasted for many years.

**A young Pancho when she was blazing
new flying records and creating legends.**

Pancho and her favorite airplane, the Travelair Mystery Ship. Howard Hughes borrowed it once, broke the prop and had it repaired without telling her. But she noticed and cussed him out as only she could.

BREAKS EARHART AIR RECORD BY FLYING 196 MILES IN HOUR

Florence Barnes Fails to Break Earhart Record

LOS ANGELES, Aug. 2 (U.P.)—Florence Lowe Barnes, prominent Southern California flier, failed late yesterday in an effort to break Amelia Earhart's world airplane speed record for women, according to Mrs. Barnes drove her plane Nikrent, official timer. 180 hart's record of 184.5 miles per hour, was made here a e

San Marino Woman Fails In Speed Test

LOS ANGELES, Aug. 2.—Florence Lowe Barnes, San Mari flier, failed yesterday in an attempt to break the world speed ord for women, when she dro low-wing monoplane over a away course here at 184.1 hour, four-tenths of a r than the mark held by hart.

FLORENCE BARNES STRIKES AUTO IN PECOS LANDING

Ruth Nichols First to Land in Midland; Phoebe Omlie, Second; and Amelia Earhart, Third

Amelia Earhart Leads 13 Girls to El Paso Control

Pasadena Aviatrix Fails To Break Air Record Held by Miss Earhart

Woman's Speed Record Broken

LOS ANGELES, Aug. 4—(U'
...ence Lowe Barnes, p...

SPEED TEST TO BE MADE FRIDAY AT AIR HARBOR

Woman Flier Will Make Attempt To Vanquish Amelia Earhart

...break Amelia
...184

upon the chief executive disarmed him.

FLORENCE BARNES NOW HOLDS WOMEN'S AIR SPEED RECORD

By United Press.
LOS ANGELES, Aug.
world's airplane

MRS. BARNES SHOWS SKILL

Attempt to Establish Ne
Mark Fails in
illing Flight

...ve F... San

Minister's Wife Holds Women's Speed Record

LOS ANGELES, Aug. 5 —(AP)
—Florence Lowe Barnes, San Marino flyer, today holds the wom-
en's speed record for airplanes.
She averaged 196.19 miles per
hour at the municipal airport
yesterday in her Travelair mystery ship, breaking the former
record of 184.6 miles per hour
set by Amelia Earhart.
Mrs. Barnes, wife of a South
Pasadena, Calif., minister, set a
new record in her first attempt
yesterday. Arriving at the field,
she notified Joe Nikrent, official
timer for the National Aeronaut-
ics association, she intended to
...y for the record and a few mi-
...s later flashed over the
course.

Amelia Earhart Loses Air Crown to Coast Woman

By United Press
Los Angeles, Aug. 5—The world's
airplane speed record for women
was claimed today by Mrs. Florence
Lowe Barnes' Pasadena aviatrix, as
the result o... ...which she
was time... ...196.1
miles a...
mile c...
Mrs...
crow...
Atla...
of...

Amelia Earhart

Right: **Pancho and a group of lady pilots. Pancho is the one on the right in the jodphurs and Amelia Earhart is in the center.**

EIGHTEEN WOMEN ENTER AIR DERBY

Ruth Elder and Mrs. Claire Fahy Two of Later Entrants for Contest

Florence Barnes Fails for Record

Florence Lowe Barnes failed in her attempt to break the world plane speed record for women yesterday in a flight over a mile course at Los Angeles municipal airport.

She averaged 180 miles an hour, according to Joe Nikrent, official timer. However, he announced that Mrs. Barnes was clocked at 190 miles an hour on one of the four laps. The record is held by Amelia Earhart, who established a mark of 184 miles an hour.

The noted Los Angeles woman flyer will attempt to shatter the record again next week.

Cigarette Sets Derby Plane Afire; Girl Crashes; Burned

FORT WORTH, Tex.

Flying Wife Of Parson Is Out of Race

Mrs. Florence Barnes Cracks Up Her Plane at Pecos

OTHERS IN MISHAPS

14 Leave Midland; Are to Spend Night at Fort Worth

Mrs. Barnes Seeks Air Speed Record

Anything faster than 185 miles an hour will be Mrs. Florence Lowe Barnes' goal this morning, when -wing Travelair over a marked nicipal Airport. seeking to better peed record for will be made

MISHAPS HIT THREE FLIERS IN AIR RACE

Sensational Flying of Amelia Earhart Features Day's Air Derby Flights

Plane Fire from Cigarette Provides Thrill for Cleveland Woman Flier

Texas, Aug. 22

WINNER IN AIR RACE

MRS. BARNES

Women Pilots Brave Fog Hazard in "Tom Th"

Seeks Record

7. (U.P.) ted Pass off at 4 to break record vel

News clips about Pancho

MRS. BARNES IS TOM THUMB DERBY VICTOR

Interest in the women's national air derby to Chicago, which starts next week from Long Beach, is expected to b~ among aero-

GIRL WILL FLY FOR SPEED OVER AIRPORT COURSE

Florence Barnes Dated To Test Record This Afternoon

MARVEL CROSSON IS KILLED WHEN PLANE CRASHES IN ARIZONA

~riz., Aug. 20.—(LP)—Tragedy entered ~erby when the body of Marvel Crosson, ~ica's best known feminine pilots, was ~reckage of her plane in wild country

NUMBER 8.

SPEED TRIAL FAILS

Florence Barnes Fails To Equal Air - speed Mark

Although t~ were flow~ the at Barn~s Los Ang win the s~ ~rix over a ~hen the ~s dropped t~ ~o laps at I record. ~e present re~ ~a Earhart for miles an hour.

LOS ANGELES, Aug. 1.—(UP)— Florence Lowe Barnes, promi- nent Southern California flier, failed late today in an effort to break Amelia Earhart's world airplane speed record for women. Mrs. Barnes drove her plane 180 miles an hour, according to Joe Nikrent, official timer. Miss Earhart's record of 184.5 miles an hour was made here a year ago.
—0—

MRS. BARNES' PLANE FALLS IN AIR DERBY

Wings Torn Off Making nding Puts Rector's Out of Derby Tex.

News clips about Pancho

A USAF photo. Photo caption stated Pancho's ranch was becoming a national historic site that day.

Posters from movies in which
Pancho and her pilots did the flying

Above: **Jean Harlow and Ben Lyon in a scene from "Hell's Angels"**, a movie in which Pancho flew. Below: Shelly Winters and many other stars made films at the Happy Bottom. Dozens more came simply to spend a weekend. Winters is surrounded here by some of the best test pilots in the world: L to R: **Capts. Jack Ridley, Jimmy Doolittle Jr., Chuck Yeager, Majors Russ Schleeh and Pete Everest.**

Battle scene from "Hell's Angels." For the sound version of this movie microphones were attached to airborne baloons and pancho and her motion picture pilots buzzed the baloons with appropriate engine and gun burst noises.

Above: A typical evening at the Happy Bottom Club. Pancho is the third from the left. Below: General Jimmy Doolittle, Pancho and actor Richard Arlen. Arlen, star of the movie "Wings" was the first to win an academy award.

A scene from the Happy Bottom Club.

Pancho and old crop duster.

Above: **The famous OX-5 engine that powered the Jennies and some of the other aircraft flown by Pancho.** Below: **A scene from the "Cisco Kid." Pancho played an important part in getting Cisco released from prison when he ran afoul of the law on trumped up charges.**

Some of Pancho's hostesses at the Happy Bottom Club

Pancho and Eugene "Mac" McKendry, Pancho's ranch foreman, companion, and later her fourth husband.

6

Pancho's previous work with the motion picture industry and her rising star as an aviatrix were an inevitable catalyst for her reentry into the movies.

In the short span of a couple of years she had become a world-renowned "Lady Pilot" and was appearing regularly in the papers and newsreels.

After the Glendale Airport became operational the first woman's air race was staged. It was open to all qualified women pilots and was flavored by a challenge from outstanding female pilot Bobbie Trout. Only Pancho and Margaret Perry met the challenge. Pancho won the race and with her usual flair for showmanship—she lapped the field.

It was expensive to compete in the air races and to fly around just for the hell of it so Pancho accepted a job with Union Oil Company to do some promotional, public relations, and executive hauling for them. She was also doing some evaluation and test work for Travelaire. With this kind of backing she entered the first women's transcontinental air race.

The race started in Santa Monica and was to end in Cleveland, Ohio, and Pancho was in there with some real pros. Among the other contestants were speed queen Amelia Earhart, beautiful Louise Thaden, Marvel Crosson, the wife of barnstormer Joe Crosson, Patty Wills, Blanche Noyes, Vera Don Walker, Marjorie Crawford, and Ruth Elder. A few years after this race it was Joe Crosson's sad duty to fly the bodies of Will Rogers and Wiley Post out of Alaska after their fatal crash at Point Barrow.

The race was disastrous for some of the contestants and Pancho did not escape without scratches. At Yuma, Arizona, the first stopover of the race, Amelia Earhart nosed her airplane over and the propeller was damaged. The race was held up until the damaged propeller was replaced. Then they proceeded to the next check point, Phoenix, Arizona. In Phoenix, Marvel Crosson complained that there was something about her plane that did not "feel right" but she couldn't put her finger on the trouble. She elected to continue in the race and was killed when her airplane crashed during the takeoff from Phoenix. Philosophically, the race went on.

"There was a lot of heavy betting on these air races and you might say that it was common practice for someone to tamper with the airplanes. Something like sponging a race horse—putting a sponge in a horse's nose to make breathing difficult to make sure that he doesn't win. Some of those tamperings were pretty serious and I was often concerned for my own safety. Those of us who trusted each other would have our airplanes guarded during overnight race stops. It was something like the old western ring of wagons except we would make a wing-tip to wing-tip circle with the noses pointed toward the center and then have one guard patrol the inside of the circle and another one on the outside. Helluva way to live but it was necessary."

Much as today, although much more prevalent, there were always the extremes of flying—supreme joy to dramatic heartbreak. After the heartbreak there had to be hope so that the flying would continue. After Pancho had been witness to the accident of Amelia Earhart and the death of her friend Marvel Crosson, she continued in the race.

"The Travelaire didn't have much visibility on the ground and you had to snake along while taxiing to steer around any obstacles. Once the tail was on the ground after a landing it was very difficult to see what was directly in front of the airplane so you just trusted to luck that there wouldn't be anyone or anything on the landing strip. After Phoenix, our next stop was Pecos, Texas, and here I really ran into trouble.

"After I was on the ground, some damned hairbrained sonovabitch drove a truck smack into the side of my airplane and knocked it for a loop. Tore up things so badly that I had to drop out of the race.

"I was doing some test flying for Travelaire at the time so they picked me up and took me to air race headquarters in Cleveland. The town was really into the spirit of air racing and we had the freedom to just about turn the town upside down. It was a custom that the people who bet on a particular pilot could kick the pilot's ass if he didn't win the race and believe me I got my ass kicked all over the hotel."

Pancho had her own story of Amelia Earhart and it certainly didn't coincide with normal public opinion. After Pancho had beaten Amelia's speed record in her Travelaire *Mystery "S"*, Amelia had written a book called *For The Fun Of It*. In a section of the book devoted to women pilots, Miss Earhart wrote words which described Pancho as a "marginal" pilot. Pancho's fury lasted for more than forty years and surely influenced her opinion of Miss Earhart.

Pancho had bought a sleek black and red Travelaire airplane dubbed the *Mystery "S"*. (It was kept a secret until the day Jimmy Doolittle won the 1931 Bendix Air Race with it.) Pancho had a couple of false starts in the *Mystery "S"* and then beat Amelia Earhart's woman's speed record. Amelia had flown 184.6 MPH and Pancho's 196.19 stood until Ruth Nichols broke it with 210 MPH.

"Amelia was married to George Putnam and he was in the book publishing and selling business. He was a businessman who could share vicariously in her adventures and make money at the same time. He was a master at his craft and was sort of a Svengali to Amelia. He'd dream up these publicity generating ideas and then send her out to do them. She was a goddamned robot. Putnam would wind her up and she'd go and do what he said. Whenever she fucked up he would scold her as a child. He kept this up until she almost lost confidence in herself so then he backed off.

"You can believe whatever you want to about what happened to Amelia but I know what happened because I heard it happen. She and Noonan just plain ran out of gas and splashed down into the ocean. Some of the Navy boys had a special radio and through some fluke of the atmosphere we picked up Amelia's last radio call. We heard her tell about being out of gas and heading for the sea. Then I heard her scream just before the radio went dead. I never have understood why they never released that story publicly but went through all of that bullshit about 'Whatever really happened to Amelia Earhart?' Hell, I know exactly what happened to her as well as I know what used to happen to Aimee Semple McPherson when she disappeared or was 'kidnapped.' "

* * *

During the "Big War" years there was a special group of people who called themselves "short snorters." It was a big fraternity and included the whole spectrum of humanity from pauper to prince. Pancho remembered that this custom started in her house in San Marino when a bunch of ragtag pilots were there and trying to figure out a way to make a few bucks.

"The short snorts were started in my home in 1928. An autographed dollar bill was the membership card. The inventors of this custom were celebrated pilots and people in the public eye, so many others wanted to join our club. We would sell them a membership for whatever amount we thought they could stand. Then the member autographed the membership dollar bill and told the new guy to go collect autographs of other fliers on the same bill, pay the stated fee, and they were then full-fledged members of the 'Short Snorters.'

"This was just a way to get money because we were all feeling the pinch of the depression. A trick of the club was for someone to stand up at a party or in a bar and call for all members to show their membership cards—the autographed dollar bill. Whoever could not produce his bill had to pay every member in the room a dollar.

"Most of the short snorters were natural hell raisers and life around them was never dull. There in Cleveland a bunch of racing pilots stole a portable organ and rode around town all night playing and singing raunchy songs.

"Although I didn't win that race, it was a good lesson and I certainly enjoyed the short snorters and the post-race activity in Cleveland."

Pancho continued racing the Speedwing and was a consistent winner.

At the height of her racing and aerial aerobatic career she was invited to come back to movieland and do some flying for pictures. Howard Hughes hired Pancho and some of her San Marino sidekicks to do the flying for the making of a soundtrack for *Hell's Angels*, and when Pancho found out what Hughes was paying his movie stunt pilots, she demanded that it be raised from $25 to $125 a day—as long as they were on location and whether they flew or not! Hughes, who was paying stars like Jean Harlow astronomical salaries, indignantly refused and a long-running gun battle with Pancho was begun.

"If he could pay some of those painted dummies who had no talent such big money, he could surely afford a hundred and twenty-five bucks a day for a pilot who risked his life doing all kinds of stupid stuff. Howard had us flying down streets, crashing into barns, spinning right down to camera level, and all kinds of shit like that. We had lots of pilots killed doing those cheap stunts. To get more pay for everyone, I formed a union.

"The Motion Picture Pilots' Association was formed with me as president. Best pilots in the world were the members, guys like Frank Clark, Ira Reed, Leo Noomis, Roy Wilson, Vince Barnett, and Paul Mantz. The union lasted forever and when the picture people started using military planes and pilots they still had to pay us. I still get a little old token check from them every now and then. The guys were so happy with the new pay scales and the union that they gave me a gold membership card.

"Like I mentioned before, Frank Clark was always my favorite but I had a full-blooded Pawnee Indian named Ira Reed who was also a lot of fun and a good man in the bedroom. Ira did a lot of flying in *Hell's Angels* and got mashed up pretty bad when he crashed while filming a scene in Taft, California. Ira came from a reservation in Oklahoma and earned money to buy his first airplane by hanging by his hair from the axle of a low-flying air show airplane. He had his hair in braids with little hooks on the ends of the braids and would crawl out of the airplane, hook the braids over the landing gear axle and then lower himself to where he was just hanging by the braids. He would stretch out his arms and have the pilot fly him at shoe-top level in front of the spectators.

"Ira was the youngest of my association and for some reason was always trying to get to sleep with me. He had an old Whippet car that would barely make it across town so one day I told Ira to run an errand for me up to Bakersfield. Before he left I told him that if he made it back by 9 P.M. that I'd be waiting for him in my bedroom because I knew that it would be an impossible task for that old Whippet. I forgot about the whole thing until I heard an uproar downstairs and then Ira, like Douglas Fairbanks, came flying through the French doors which led to the balcony. He thrust his watch in front of me and it was exactly 9 P.M. Ira and I had a lot of fun and I often regretted not getting started with him a bit sooner.

"While they were making *Hell's Angels*, Ira sort of developed an infatuation for Jean Harlow. She was always very nice to him and when they would have lunch together in the commissary there was always some wag who called them Beauty and the Beast. Whenever Schulberg and Robbins came out with books about Harlow, Ira was mad enough to kill them because he thought that they had misrepresented her and painted a bad image of her. Ira later raced horses and taught a lot of racing people like Eddie Arcaro how to fly. I loved that crazy Indian and wish that there were more like him.

Many years after his movie and wartime flying ended, Ira Reed had a flying service at Taos, New Mexico. One day he and I were flying a Cessna 195 from Taos to Albuquerque and were following the Rio Grande. Ira would go below the river banks and just skip above the water's edge.

"There's a lot of bridges and wires across the river, Ira," I cautioned, "you'd better get higher."

"No sweat, know them all," he growled.

At that moment a half-completed bridge loomed before us. Ira pulled up abruptly, cleared the bridge and then settled back close to the water. Unruffled, he cast his wrinkled old eyes toward me.

"All but one, that is," he laughed.

Ira was a great pilot and a colorful character. When he died, four beautiful ladies flew from Los Angeles to Taos for the funeral. Each one seemed alone and each one was dressed in exquisite black dresses with thin black veils. They sat apart from one another during the funeral ceremony and each one wept softly. At the end of the simple eulogy, while four Indians tapped softly on tom-toms, each of these ladies put a bouquet of red roses on Ira's casket and left the church. None of them spoke to anyone nor to each other and they left Taos in complete mystery.

One evening while attending a meeting of a flying fraternity called the 'Quiet Birdmen', Ira Reed and I had a table close to the bar. A Navy admiral, resplendent in uniform, buttons, ribbons, and bows, was telling a captive audience about his flying and career exploits.

" 'You know, I graduated from the University of Illinois, the best technical school in the world," the admiral bragged.

Ira looked over his shoulder and growled, 'Hey sailor-boy, what the hell do you think MIT stands for, Massachusetts Institute of *Theology?*'

The admiral ignored Ira and continued, "Had I chosen, I would have continued in the field of test flying but I felt I would be more valuable in other pursuits."

" 'You big phoney. You never flew anything bigger than 40-horsepower and you were afraid to get out of the traffic pattern with that,' Ira taunted.

The admiral reddened and told Ira that any more of his remarks would call for some kind of physical retribution.

Ira rose and thrust his Indian-nickel look-alike face into the florid one of the admiral.

" 'Great," Ira thundered, "Take your best shot, then I'm going to break off your gold braided arm and shove it up your fucking ass."

The admiral left in a huff.

* * *

Ira was married to a beautiful blonde lady who shared his love for the outdoor adventuresome life and when she was killed in an accident, Ira took refuge in his Indian heritage. He would let his hair grow long, dress in elegant Western-style clothing, drench himself in heavy turquoise and silver jewelry and wear an outrageous high-crowned black hat pulled low over his eyes. Thus attired, he would wander about the country visiting old friends.

During one of these Indian periods, Ira was in a hospital coffee shop during a visit to my wife who was hospitalized and was seated across the counter from four middle-aged women whose breakfasts had just been served. A group of nurses came into the shop at that moment and created a bit of noise with their chatter and laughter.

"You would think that they, of all people, would realize that this is a hospital and would be more reserved and quiet," one of the blue-haired ladies observed.

"Certainly would," another of the ladies agreed. "They sound like a pack of wild Indians."

Ira, with his tall black hat pulled low over his brow, stared at them with obsidian eyes. "And how in the fuck would you know what a wild Indian would sound like?" he demanded.

For the first time the women saw the obviously outraged Indian across from them and they were terrified. Ira's choice of language didn't help matters and the combination of the man and his threatening, obscene vocabulary caused the four women to rush from the restaurant, their breakfasts untouched and their bills unpaid.

* * *

Frank Clark, a Clark Gable look-alike, was Pancho's favorite. She never spoke of Frank without getting that far-away look of the eternal romantic in her eyes. I suspect that Frank was the real love of Pancho's life although he was not included among her four husbands.

"The 1929-1930 era was so full of wonderful and exciting people and things that they pop out like separate episodes. It was full of flying, romancing, brawls, parties, meeting wonderful people, traveling all over the U.S. and Mexico that it descends on me as just one glorious dream. It was the wonderful era of Frank Clark.

"Frank was a descendant of the early Spanish that came sailing into San Francisco Bay. He was one of the greatest characters who ever flew. He was a very strange person. We called him 'Spook' because he had an ability to know a lot of things by instinct, what we now call extrasensory perception. I have a bit of that myself, but Spook really had it. If I called him on the phone he'd always answer, 'Hello, Pancho,' before I said a word. The power that Frank had over people was out of this world. We didn't think that it was hypnotism but somehow or another he always had people groveling at his feet. Everyone loved Frank but a lot of people were jealous of him. He always had an idea that Paul Mantz hated his guts but Paul loved him just like everybody else.

"Frank had some mean little characters in the form of some tiny carved beans he had picked up in South America. One of these, called Little Joe, was supposed to be really powerful and would allow Frank to put a 'spell' on people. One afternoon while we were all loafing around on movie locations, one of the guys started daydreaming about a South Pacific island where we should all go. He drew out this island on a piece of paper and designed the 'safe harbor' for all of us. We would all have float planes and each one would have a private cove of the island for his own use. Each one would have his own house and in the center of the island there would be a community club and bar. Each one of us chose our imaginary cove and mentally designed our house.

The whole thing was make-believe but it looked good on paper.

"Frank Clark walked in and after the plan was explained to him he selected a cove that had previously been chosen by an airmail pilot. They argued over who should have that particular make-believe cove and Frank threatened to put a 'curse' on the other pilot if he didn't relinquish his claim. He stood firm so Frank rubbed Little Joe and announced that the airmail pilot was now hexed and that every time he flew he would have an accident. He had nine consecutive accidents and the mail was not getting through so the Department of Commerce wrote Frank Clark a letter on official government stationery directing him to remove the hex. Frank replied that he only knew how to put on hexes and not take them off so the accidents continued.

"Frank was like an airplane and could be treated rough without falling apart, but at other times the slightest abuse would destroy him. I adored him. I was his shadow. He was the most exciting man in my life. He was not boy friend or sweetheart but someone I loved and wanted to be around all of the time.

"Back before I knew him, Frank was a rumrunner—not by air but by truck. He and his pals brought booze from San Francisco to Los Angeles and it was in Los Angeles where Frank had his faithful girl friend, Olive. After the long night's run, Olive always had tasty ham and egg breakfasts ready for the boys. She was a wonderful person.

"Frank had such an apparent slaphappy way of doing things that one didn't actually realize that he lived a carefully planned life and knew exactly what he was doing every minute. The part of his character that appeared to be slap-happy and offbeat was only part of his flair and outgoing personality.

"Frank was really a softie at heart but he thought that he was the meanest man alive. Whenever he got drunk he became sentimental and cried. But he also had a latent brutal streak. He used to fly with a man called Hugh Kimmel who was a cop and sported a long flowing beard. Hugh used to fly the hell out of his Jenny with his beard flowing behind him like the silk scarves of other pilots. Frank and Hugh got into some kind of donnybrook and Hugh took a shot at Frank which missed. He then gave his .45 to Frank and told him that it was his turn to shoot at him. The gun was Hugh's prized possession and he had neat little notches carved in the handle for each man he had killed. Frank wouldn't shoot Hugh but he threw the gun to the pavement and broke the carved handle. Hugh broke out in tears and Frank was so moved that he started crying too. There, sitting on the running board of a car, were two tough guys crying over nothing.

"Although they were sentimental, these guys played rough. During a fight, Hugh broke Frank's jaw and Frank bent Hugh's arm behind his back until it broke. Then they both cried and, arm-in-arm, went to the hospital to get the damage repaired."

Frank survived a lot of things and was finally killed in a Bt-13 when he buzzed a silver mine in the Mojave Desert. He and a couple of partners owned the mine and had a miner/caretaker who stayed at the mine full time. There wasn't room to land an airplane there so Frank would drop supplies from the air. He would first buzz the mine to let the miner know that he was there and then would drop the supplies. On the fateful day of his death he made a low pass, pulled up to turn back in for the supply drop, and flew into the ground. An investigation showed that his fuel tanks were empty.

The incidence of fatal accidents in the movie stunt pilot business was exceptionally high and the ranks of the Motion Picture Pilots' Association were decimated quite rapidly. Whenever a pilot was killed there was an Irish wake and a big "gangster-type" funeral. Most of these events were celebrated in the Beverly Hills Hotel where Pancho and her renegades stayed while working on a film.

"During one of these lavish funerals, sort of a pagan tradition anyway, we got to thinking about how stupid it was to make such a big deal *after* the guy was dead. We decided to have a funeral for each one of us *before* we got killed. We took the names alphabetically and whenever we had the opportunity we would have a funeral. There would be a fucking big party at the Beverly Hills Hotel and the chosen corpse would be the guest of honor. There was a big rest-in-peace floral piece of white carnations in the lobby and limousines filled with flowers outside. After the party was over, we'd all drive out to the cemetery and during a mock "ashes to ashes" delivered by a real preacher, would donate the flowers and wreaths to somebody's grave. After that, if the honoree was killed, there would be only a simple ceremony of the basics of a burial. Once in a while somebody would get killed before we had his 'funeral' and we'd have to go back to the old way of doing things.

"Along about this time I was living at movie director Eric Von Stroheim's and doing some script writing for him. He was every bit the taskmaster he looked to be. Whenever I did something wrong he would be the goddamned field marshall and just raise holy hell. One night I had worked my ass of rewriting somebody's lousy script and when I gave it to Von Stroheim he exploded. He banged a riding crop on a desk until the whole house rattled and told me to get up to my 'office' and write a decent script. Wasn't a fucking thing wrong with that script, just that asshole throwing his weight around. I went upstairs and brooded until the evening, then I made a rope out of sheets and left by the balcony outside my room. I met Frank Clark and some of the guys and we had a hell-raising night on the town. I sneaked back in about dawn and when I heard Von Stroheim yelling for his breakfast I strolled down the stairs carrying the same script, not a goddamned word changed. Von Stroheim looked at my red eyes, haggard face, and generally worn out appearance and figured I'd worked all night on his fucking script. He read through it quickly, said it was excellent, and a good example of what a little hard work could produce. I laughed all the way back to the bedroom where I then slept all day."

Pancho's experiences with the darlings of the movies during the era of the "Silver Screen" evoke some of her most animated memories.

"Ramon Navarro was a real Latin heartbreaker. Everywhere he went the women trailed him like a bunch of dogs chasing a bitch in heat. Funny how much of an animal we really are and we try so damned hard to always deny and hide that relationship. Ramon and I became a real "number" around Hollywood, zooming around in one of his high-powered cars or chasing about on horseback. He did everything for me, bought clothes, flowers, jewelry and all of the romantic stuff.

"Ramon had a special flying outfit made for me in Brazil. It was of light blue soft suede and consisted of pants, jacket and helmet. He had a pair of soft leather Brazilian boots made to go along with it and a pale powder-blue silk scarf. It was a dramatic outfit and I loved it. One day at Glendale airport we were all gathered for some event and as usual Roscoe Turner was there with his fucking lion Gilmore. While we were all talking, Gilmore pissed on those beautiful boots Ramon had given me and I was infuriated. I grabbed Turner's riding crop and started after Gilmore and Turner started after me yelling for me to leave Gilmore alone. One of the newsreel companies was there, Pathe or Movietone or somebody, and the theater news of the next week was that scene of Roscoe, Gilmore and me. Whoever narrated it didn't have the guts to tell what started the whole thing.

"These were truly magnificent people and it's too goddamned bad that so many of them passed from the scene while other unimaginative people who don't do a fucking thing in their entire lives live forever. There has to be a reason and we'll probably know why someday but right now all that we can do is bitch and wonder."

It ain't changed, Pancho.

---------------------------- **7** ----------------------------

With her successes in flying and motion pictures, Pancho had learned a lot about people, places, and politics. So she decided to run for Supervisor of the Third District of Los Angeles County. She felt that the Pancho name tag was a bit frivolous for a politician so she campaigned as Florence Lowe Barnes.

"I put a smoke generator on the Speedwing and took advantage of a piece of equipment that the other politicians didn't have by writing my name in the sky every afternoon. Skywriting is really not very difficult because everything is done on the horizontal instead of the vertical. It's easy to see where you have been and what you have done so if you don't spell very well you simply write the words on a piece of paper on the instrument panel and then cross out each word after you have written it. You don't even have to think. In the old ships we would write downhill; in other words, we'd end up at a lower altitude than where we started. This was to be able to do it quickly so that the wind wouldn't blow away the first letters before we'd written the last.

"I lost the election but my friend, Buron Fitts, won as Los Angeles District Attorney and he was bone-tired after a fabulous and victorious campaign. One of the attorneys in his office called and we set up a trip to Mexico. It was a funny request, because all through the campaign I'd been kidding him. I'd always razz him from the platform when he was making his speeches and it was probably because I didn't take anything too seriously, including or perhaps particularly, politics. I did have myself an awful lot of fun and I used to razz Buron because he blushed so easily. He was a very strong and opinionated man and people were always taking verbal potshots at him during the election. Sometimes the shots were real. I never knew of his being hostile toward the bootleggers or anyone else so I couldn't figure why anyone would want to shoot him. He always had a heavy bodyguard and a few bullet holes in his car.

"When we took off for Mexico, Buron was armed with all sorts of artillery. I told him that he wasn't going with me as long as he carried a gun and after a long verbal battle he agreed to go unarmed. He was worried and told me that it was up to me to protect him. I told him not to worry because no one else in the United States and no one else in Mexico gave a shit about the District Attorney of Los Angeles. He was so used to the hell of Los Angeles that he could not visualize the peace and tranquility of Mexico.

"Once the decision to go was made, Buron wanted to leave right away so with my cousin Dean as messenger, we pulled all of the skywriting equipment off of the airplane and headed for Phoenix. I could never understand his goddamned hurry for we were in a 100-mile-per-hour-airplane which really isn't going anywhere in a hurry when you're starting out on a several thousand mile trip. When we got to Phoenix we stayed at the classy Westward-Ho Hotel. There was always a joke about that place that said that all of the bus drivers and taxi pilots who met the trains would yell, 'All aboard for the Westward-Ho House' and their vehicles were always filled to overflowing.

"I had a bunch of oil company and ferry pilot friends in Phoenix so we got together with them. With all of the bloody murders that have since been committed most readers probably won't remember Ruth Judd who had murdered a couple of young girls and shipped their bodies from Phoenix to Los Angeles in a trunk. Anyway, Buron had to use his influence for us to meet Ruth Judd. One thing that I always loved about him was that there was never a dull moment around him. He was always doing something, an exciting man and I enjoyed being in one some of the fringes of his activities.

"After leaving Phoenix we got to El Paso, Texas, the next evening and Buron wanted to cross over into Mexico immediately. He didn't realize the game of protocol that was necessary to fly an airplane into Mexico. This consisted mainly of playing checkers and drinking tequila with the Mexican immigration officials. I went down to the border and played a few games and then told them that my boss was going to make it difficult for me if I didn't get my papers straightened out that night. I told them that I knew that I couldn't get the papers fixed that night so I would just have to take whatever baloney the boss dished out. Hell, those Mexican guys had the papers fixed up and stamped in about fifteen minutes. We then relaxed and had a few sips of vino along with some more checker playing and I told them that I sure was glad that we could go on into Mexico without waking the immigration boys up at dawn.

"We flew from El Paso to Chihuahua right down on the railroad tracks. It rained and oh, how it rained. Great goddamned sheets of water. When we got there the airport looked like a lake. I could see about where I should land but couldn't tell whether the water was two feet or two inches deep. Everything below me was still, the train tracks and highways were washed out and the towns gutted with people trying to escape the ravages of the downpour. Unrelenting, that's a damn good word for that fucking rain. Me and that airplane seemed to be the only things moving in Mexico.

"I sized up the situation and figured well, hell, the only thing to do was to come in with the tail real low and drag the tail in the water to keep from nosing over if the wheels hit deep water first. I dropped the tail and down we went. The landing wasn't bad at all and everything worked out splendidly. The water was about six inches deep and when the ship hit, it made a beautiful splash and spray but no harm was done.

"To me it is strange how one remembers small details after so many years. The breakfast we had the next morning in Chihuahua was eggs rancheros where they put sunny-side up fried eggs on a tortilla and smother it with an onion, tomatoes and chile sauce. It was a wonderful breakfast and for some reason I'll always remember it as one of the extra delights of the trip.

"After breakfast we took off for San Luis Obispo but we hit some terrific head winds and got so low on gas that we had to sit down near some town on the Texas border. We sat and waited until the inevitable sweet little Mexican came along and agreed to use his burros to bring us some gasoline. This was going to take several hours because burro travel isn't too rapid and Buron had a fit about the delay. He threatened to walk to a town if I didn't take off for somewhere and I told the edgy little bastard to walk. He started out walking but within thirty minutes was back and sitting under a bush bitching about the whole situation. Eventually the gas arrived and we continued our trip for a very long day.

"The next day we made it into Mexico City at about midnight in a heavy rain. It was cold and shivery in the mountain air. The elevation at Mexico City is about 7000 feet and I came in at about 10,000 just to be safe. We were chilled and Buron who was constantly suffering with a leg injury was shivering with chills and fever.

"I was always angry about something back in those days and at this moment it was because of the people who criticized Buron about his leg injury and saying that he used it for sympathy to get votes. This was a fucking lie because he was one of the gamest men I ever knew. I love pure guts and Buron had them. Soon as we would hit a hotel he would start working on some of the problems facing him when he got back to Los Angeles. Although he was suffering from the leg problem and a high fever, he refused to relax and rest.

"After we landed at Mexico City I had put the airplane in the hangar at the Pan American airport which was the main municipal airport. I didn't understand the furor but the Mexican Air Corps people were really unhappy with me because I had not landed at the military airfield. They took me in their car and we went to get my airplane. The Mexican officers would not allow any of the Pan-Am mechanics to touch my airplane. They personally wheeled it out of the hangar. It was only a hop across the strip to the military field and before we moved the airplane, I wanted to pay the night's hangar rent but the officers told me that I owed the

Americans absolutely nothing. Besides that, they didn't like the Americans but they did like me. Once we got over to the Mexican Army Air Field they really made a fuss over me.

"At their field the Mexicans practically took my ship apart and then put it back together in perfect condition. They replaced plugs, cleaned everything in the engine, fueled the tanks, changed the oil and had the ship ready to go.

"I had wanted Buron to stay at one of the old hotels but he insisted on a newer and more respectable place. I had a room of my own at the hotel and the Air Corps guys all crowded into it. Although it was against the rules for lady guests to have male visitors, the Air Corps boys fixed that up with a few pesos and soon they were drinking toasts to me and we had a helluva time.

"I was getting the red carpet treatment and felt that Buron was being neglected so I set out to show him the town. I took him out expecting him to want to hit the Red Mill or Green Mill or whatever the hell it was—the Garibaldi, that was the name of the joint. When we got there, I found it was for men only and they wouldn't let me in. Although I had on jodhpur boots, pants and a jacket like a man, a grouchy pock-marked Mexican man refused to let me in. The next night I wore the uniform of a full Mexican Air Corps colonel and along with us we had a bunch of goodwill flyers from Cuba. As we filed past this leering little pock-marked bastard, I couldn't help from pushing at his face with the heel of my hand. The Mexicans wanted me to really work him over but I'm not a mean person by nature and the little push was enough to get even for the ill-treatment of the night before.

"This joint was sort of a burlesque and strip tease show and we had a box seat. It seems that Mexico was under some kind of martial law at the time and that the Air Corps was about the highest command in the country. The Air Corps was the most daring and romantic of the services and enjoyed a great deal of prestige. I was scared to death wearing one of their uniforms because I didn't speak enough Spanish to bluff my way out of even a simple situation.

"As we did the town, we paid for nothing. We went to shows, restaurants, cabarets, theaters, and ate the finest of foods but never paid for anything. Even my Mexican Air Corps style haircut was free. There was a barber at the old Reyes Hotel in view of the restaurant and people would sit at the lunch counter and criticize the way that the barber was cutting hair and giving shaves.

"But to go back, the show at the Garibaldi was wild. From our box the officers I was with started throwing money on the stage—bidding for the girls' clothes and then for the girls themselves. If you won a bid you could carry the nude girl from the stage to your box and she was yours for the night. Although I was only an observer and didn't bid for the girls, it was one helluva wild night.

"Colonel Leone was with us as was General C.B. whose full name I choose not to remember. Leone always called me his cuate, or twin, a symbolic phrase for a close and loved friend. General C.B. was from a very famous Mexican family and was a giant of a man, standing about six feet four inches and with the build of a powerful athlete. He had lost an ear in a bull fighting accident and it gave him a ruffian-like appearance. This ruggedly handsome man made an entertaining specialty of eating the pants off of girls—not playing at it but actually eating the silky underpants from some good-looking broad's body. He did his act in the box at the Garibaldi that night and the crowd went wild. At a party at my house in San Marino he had eaten the filmy lace underpants from a Hollywood blonde and created a mild sensation. His wasn't just an act, for he really ate them and he did the same thing with light bulbs and other assorted things. It was a goddamned shame that he later died of pneumonia because you wouldn't expect such a colorful character to die like that. He should have had a more exciting and beautiful passing away than mere pneumonia which is a prosaic sort of death.

"The Mexican Air Corps officers took me to some swell cabarets. In one of them I met a young man I knew who had married a classmate of mine in the posh Bishop School at La Jolla. He knew me quite well but he didn't recognize me in the Mexican flier's uniform and I thought it best not to try to explain the situation to him. At the time I saw him I was busy bouncing a beautiful habitue of the demi-monde on my knee and keeping up the image and tradition of the Mexican Air Corps. The officers taught me a lot of words in Spanish and most of them were bad. I knew enough bad words in English but the addition of a few in Spanish added to the flair. These guys had a vernacular which was the crude, rough language of the pilots of Mexico but was totally unacceptable in normal Mexican company. I learned this language and the pilots would create a situation where I would say some of these words in mixed society. The women blushed and the men laughed like hell. They used me as sort of a clown to do these things they'd like to do but didn't dare. We put in about a week of hard carousing without hardly ever going to bed. Everyone did a lot more drinking than I and when it came time to meet President Rodriguez who was the president of Mexico, everyone except me was in terrible shape.

"The meeting with the president was a very formal and dramatic affair. We were all individually introduced to the president and there was an inordinate amount of bowing and scraping going on. The guest of honor was a captain who commanded the pilots from Cuba who were on a goodwill tour. The captain stood erect and while giving a military salute to the president, he collapsed in a huddle on the floor.

After we picked him up and revived him, the event became a little less formal because the president was right in there helping us. I was then introduced to President Rodriguez, a man whom I had admired for many years. The dinner was magnificent, not California-style Mexican food, but filet mignon and a lot of French dishes like you see in places like Chile. I was the only woman present and I thoroughly enjoyed the toasts, speeches, food, drink, and the overwhelming hospitality of the Mexicans.

"After this wild week and diplomatic activity in Mexico City, Buron was ready to haul ass out of there—thank God it wasn't in the middle of the night like his usual time for making snap decisions. I usually did everything that he suggested because I hadn't learned to fight with him yet and he had me slightly over-awed. Whenever I was working for someone, I always did what they told me and kinda forged ahead on an assignment like the charge of the Light Brigade. Buron gave the order and I intended following it even if we busted our asses.

"We took of in a light rain and little information on the weather ahead of us. When we got into the mountains it was raining like a son of a bitch. We made our way to Guadalajara, got gas there and took off again. We hit a solid cloud bank and although I knew the territory fairly well from the 1927 trip, I sorta circled the area trying to decide what to do. Everything beneath me was flooded and clouds surrounded me like a band of movie Indians attacking a wagon train. There was no way that I could see where we could get down in one piece so I decided to go up."

Airplanes of that era had very little in the way of instruments and some pilots disdained adding them because they preferred to fly "by the seat of the pants." Anybody who couldn't tell when they were going up or down or whether they were upside down shouldn't be there in the first place, was the attitude. Many years after this episode of which Pancho tells, Ira Reed would take me aloft in a T-6 or a Cessna 195 and get me totally disoriented in clouds or above cloud banks.

"O.K. Junior Birdman, straighten us out and get us home. You've got enough goddamned dials and shit there in front of you to fly blind to France and back," he would taunt.

I watched Ira scare the living hell out of one of the nation's leading supersonic test pilots when he demonstrated his "seat of the pants" techniques. After landing, Ira told the shaken pilot, "Don't worry about it, son. You've got lots of gauges and stuff. Your only problem is that you don't have any balls."

Pancho had the balls!

"I had no blind flying instruments but I knew that airplane and cockpit like I knew my own bed. I took that old bi-plane in a climbing turn, holding steady rotor (prop), watching my airspeed, watching the tachometer, and particularly watching my key chain which I had hung on the instrument panel as a turn and bank indicator. I wanted lots of altitude so if I fucked up and got into a spin I'd have some room for recovery. We went up through 12,000 feet of pure clouds and then broke out on top. After we were on top, I turned west and after awhile we hit a clear spot where I could look down and see the ocean. That was my cue, all that I needed, so I let down through the hole and leveled out when I had a clear view of the beach. After an eternity I made it to Mazatlan. I put that sweet little airplane on the ground and we grabbed a taxi to the old Belmar Hotel.

"The Belmar was a nice old hotel in the best tradition of Mexico. We had landed at the only field that was there and they had some of the "sensitive" plants there. I loved to play with these plants. If you reach out to touch them, they will shrink away from you and the leaves will fold up. These plants always pleased me because they were so much alive and like people.

"Buron was ready to fold when we got to the hotel so I let him fold. I was unhappy with him because it was to be his last night in Mexico and I thought we ought to raise a little more hell before leaving the country. While exploring the town on my own, I found a couple of beautiful Mexican girls with gorgeous big tits and I talked them into going back to the hotel with me. The girls were afraid to go into the hotel but I finally convinced them that it was O.K. so they went with me. Goddamned Buron didn't even want to talk to them so I sent them back in a taxi and went for a walk along the south beach.

"After all of that lousy flying weather, the sky had cleared and it was an artist's night on the beach. Tranquility, blue water, white sand, and a moon that made the whole scene as if lighted by an expert movie light technician.

"I took off all of my clothes, placed them in a neat pile on the beach and went into the water. I'm not much of a swimmer or a beach nut, but the combination of palm trees, moonlight and gorgeous beach made it impossible to resist the gentle blue water. When I came out of the water I found a young man sitting next to my pile of clothes.

" 'It is not permitted to swim without a suit, and it is not permitted to swim after two o'clock,' he said in slow Spanish.

"I told him that I was sorry and that I was just a dumb gringa who did not know the rules. He told me that it was O.K. and that he was just sitting there to make sure that no one stole my clothes. He rose and bowed and treated me as an elegant lady rather than as a naked hoodlum doing forbidden things.

"I could see the wonderful long sweep of his dark eyelashes and the sparkle in his deep brown eyes. He was tall and had broad shoulders. He was so elegantly formal in view of my nudity that I couldn't bear to shatter all of his fine dignity or I believe that I would have simply grabbed him and ripped his clothes off on that beach. He handed me my clothing while I got dressed and then escorted me back to the hotel.

"I wish that everybody in the United States could know what nice people the Mexicans really are. Americans go to Mexico and act like horses' asses and heels. They throw their money around and think that buys them the right to insult people and behave as they wish. Of course, the Mexicans have grown used to it for some of them live from the tourist dollar. We certainly don't make friends in Mexico and the Mexicans don't like us because we treat them like scum when actually there is not a finer, more polite, lovely nation than that of Mexico. I dearly love the Mexican people.

"The next day was a bitch. Eighteen hours of flying and it was about the roughest day I ever put in in the air. We took off in bad weather and it stayed that way. It was dreadfully, dreadfully hot, the sun came through the clouds, and beat down on me from time to time and I think that I almost suffered a heat stroke. I had spilled some gas on myself during servicing and the combination of the skin burns from the gasoline and the hot sun made life miserable.

"We cleared the border at Nogales, Arizona, and it started for Gila Bend when the instrument panel lights went out and I started experiencing a case of vertigo. I kept feeling that the airplane was in a slow turn to the right and

67

starting to roll. I spotted a train with a bright headlight, got my orientation straightened out and headed for the lights of the Imperial Valley. We landed at the desert town of Indio and had a big steak with all the trimmings. We called my house from Indio and Blackie—one of my pilots who got that nickname from Howard Hughes—told us that we could probably make it on in but that the weather was getting steadily worse. Usually my boys were better predictors of weather than the weather service but this time they were wrong and by the time we got to the Los Angeles Basin it was just one big solid pack of clouds. I didn't want Buron to pay for gas that he wasn't going to use so I didn't put in much at Indio. That proved to be stupid. The combination of weather and low fuel caused me to try to locate March Field at Riverside and to land there.

"The fog was thick and while I was on top of it I could not even see the mountains that surround March Field. Then I saw a glow on the clouds from the March Field beacon and knew where I was because I knew to a gnat's eyebrow where that beacon was located. I lined up my approach pattern with the beacon as reference, came in low with lots of power, pulled power off, pulled the nose up, and let the ship come down for a three-point landing like it was standing on three legs. It was a totally blind situation and very scary. After the landing I was overwrought with nervous strain, physical exhaustion, and the fatigue of the long hours. A soldier came out and tried to direct me by walking by the wingtip but the ground fog was so thick that I ran into a tent and bent the propeller. Together, the soldier and I pushed the airplane into the hangar. I called home and they sent a car to pick us up and the great Mexican adventure was over.

"Several weeks later, after the propeller had been repaired, I went to March Field to get the plane. While taxiing to the fuel pumps the engine quit for lack of gas which meant that we landed with only a couple of minutes of fuel in the tanks. That was scary and one of those things that in retrospect makes you realize how close you came to killing yourself and whoever might be with you—really gives you wet pants and the collywobbles."

8

Things were getting tough for everybody in 1931 and Pancho was not spared. She and her high-flying buddies were still doing their movie parts to pick up a few bucks but their jobs became pretty scarce. The mansion in San Marino was only a facade for the declining fortunes inside, and all of the party participants had to also be contributors. It was a "bring your own" when they had a big dinner and the guests would bring the ingredients for the meal.

The decline of their fortunes didn't make the hell raisin' barnstormers lose their sense of humor or adventurousness.

"We made a picture called *Cocks of the Air* and the goddamned censors were so stuffy about it that we changed it to *Penises of the Ozone.*"

Pancho did some maximum weight takeoff tests for Lockheed and they used a dry lake bed in the Mojave Desert for a runway. The floor of the lake bed was like packed concrete. It ran for sixteen miles and takeoffs and landings could be made in any direction. The lake was named Muroc Dry Lake because of one of the bureaucratic peculiarities of our times. A family named Corum had settled on the edge of the lake bed and somehow or another had managed to build enough of a small community to warrant a U.S. Post Office. When they made the postal request they were advised that they could not name their little town after themselves and so they reversed the spelling of their name—Corum— and the community with the dry lake was officially named Muroc.

Here, on this lonely, wind-swept, dusty, God-forsaken stretch of alkali, Pancho and Lockheed started what was to eventually become the Flight Test Center of the United States, and the birthplace of the world's greatest aircraft.

The desert around the lake bed was heavily populated with joshuas, cactus-like formations like nonsymmetrical, thorn bearing trees whose regal presence dominated the silhouette of the landscape against the clear blue sky. These trees were symbolic of the type of people who were attracted to Muroc. They were tough, independent, resistant to man's attacks on their being, and no two were alike. The individuality of the trees mirrored that of the men and women.

With irrigation and care, the desert land would produce abundant crops and alfalfa was one of the most responsive to the desert environment. Cotton, sugar beets, onions and maize also responded well to the desert earth when generously sprinkled with water. The water table beneath this arid land was only two to three hundred feet so it was not a major undertaking to drill wells to provide the necessary water for successful farming. It just took a helluva lot of hard work.

Pancho was not a farmer but she was a confidante of animals and nature so she hedged the loss of her fortune by trading a high tone apartment house in Los Angeles for 80 acres of this desert land. Her "farm" was sandwiched between Muroc Dry Lake and another one named Rosamond Dry Lake. It was a forlorn place of desolation and loneliness. It was a magnificent place of enchanted isolation.

"When my son Billy and I first got that place there wasn't anything around except coyotes, lizards, jackrabbits, and sidewinder snakes."

In 1933 Pancho and her son Billy Barnes, then about 12 years old, moved to their farm in the Mojave Desert, about 100 miles northeast of her San Marino mansion but a million miles away from the life-style of the grand house. There was a small four-toom house on the place and little else. Pancho and Billy, all alone, expanded the house, built fences, corrals, and outbuildings. The 80 acres were planted in alfalfa.

"After awhile it became obvious that the 80 acres wasn't enough to make enough bucks to live on so with a little horse trading, I parlayed the ranch into almost 400 acres and Billy and I really went to work."

This lady of wealth, fame, and the trappings of luxurious living, together with her 12-year-old son, challenged the hostile, unforgiving elements of the vacant Mojave. They expanded the house, added cows, pigs, and horses, and planted more crops. They made it into a good-paying business while most of the depression-plagued nation went begging.

A few miles from Pancho's ranch the U.S. Army had started that which was to become the world's most sophisticated Flight Test Center. But in 1933, sophisticated it was not. A contingent of seventeen Army men who christened themselves "The Foreign Legion of the American Army" were "stuck" in the middle of the dry lake bed to evaluate the value of sand-filled and cement practice bombs. The sand-filled bombs were metal carcasses filled with sand and a ten-pound black powder spotting charge. The cement bombs had metal tail fins tacked on and carried the ten-pound black powder spotting charge. The performance of these bombs was absolutely unpredictable. They were being tested so that they could be used for practice and training in lieu of the expensive real bombs.

"The sand bombs weren't too bad but those fucking concrete things went so far awry that they terrorized the whole countryside. They were dropped from several different altitudes and those from ten to twelve thousand feet shimmied through the skies like a talented belly dancer. When they hit that heated desert floor, they'd bounce all over hell, over farmland, through dairy barns, and sometimes would end up in the farmers' chicken coops.

"Those kids who were doing the testing had it really rough. First, they were living in tents and eating from sand-filled field kitchens and just about out of touch with the rest of humanity. They had some electricity but it was shut off at nine o'clock and that left them without even a light to read or write by. They always treated me swell. Many nights I stayed over there just shooting the bull with these kids and then I'd have all kinds of trouble finding my way home in the dark. They finally built a barracks big enough for sixty-four men and then there was always room for me to stay the night when I got caught there after nine o'clock. There wasn't any foolishness between me and the kids. We were just damned good pals.

"I really started the first Post Exchange for these army men by giving them one of my big red pigs to sell for raising some money. They sold it for $34 and then those dog-faced wild men blew the thirty-four bucks in a crap game. That taught me, and when we got some more dough, I started a PX and I handled the money.

"They got their exchange going finally and we would trade stuff back and forth like the old barter system. I'd started a pretty good dairy by that time and when I'd deliver the milk, I'd trade it for stuff from their PX. Always spent a lot of time around the PX batting the breeze with the guys. The guys would often come over to my place to bring some vegetables and stuff to put in my ice boxes because they didn't have refrigeration. We'd drink a bit of good wine and sit around shooting the bull till all hours. That part was always bubbles and bull.

"About this same time I watched the first experiments with night triangulation bombing that were ever made. Bombs were thrown all over the desert but there was a pilot who was a real dead-eye Dick and he pinpointed the target every time. Many of the latter-day sky-warriors owe these Muroc Foreign Legionnaires a lot of thanks, for they sure made the war-time bombing missions into a real science.

"Everything wasn't fun and games and some of these boys paid the highest price. I remember the first airplane crash at Muroc, at least it was the first crash of a military plane. One of the real crackerjack pilots was trying to land down at March Field but it was too foggy there so he headed back to Muroc. Something went wrong and he crashed into the ground while trying to make the landing. The airplane burst into violent flames and the crew struggled to free themselves from the burning wreckage. One man ran screaming across the desert on legs that were just burning stumps. He died while running. Yeah, there was always some of those sad things, nothing is ever all white.

"But things were happening in the world and Muroc kept on growing and so did my little house. With my own hands I knocked out some walls, pushed things about a bit, and before long I had a nice roomy place. I built an outside dining room, an inside dining room, patio, more bedrooms, and added a swimming pool. It got to be such a nice and attractive place that everyone wanted to move in.

"By 1935 Billy and I were pretty comfortable. We had about $1200 a month coming in from farm products and the milk business. I sold milk to the boys at Muroc, Pacific Borax Company, and then expanded to Mojave and China Lake. Our expenses were only about $500 a month so we had a neat profit of $700 and nowhere to spend it."

Pancho didn't divorce herself from flying when she took up the less glamorous pursuit of farming, and the Mojave ranch had a beautiful flying field. She stayed in touch with all of her flying and movie buddies and the ranch was sort of a hideaway for many of these old friends.

One of Pancho's movie and horseback riding friends was an actor who used the stage name of Duncan Rinaldo. Duncan was the "Cisco Kid" and I can remember many Saturdays when I sneaked into a Baltimore movie to see the "Cisco Kid" on his magnificent white horse. Duncan's real name was Visile Dumitree Cughienas and when he went to Africa to do a part in the movie, *Trader Horn*, he did not sign his real name to his passport. For this indiscretion he was doing time in McNeil Island penitentiary. Pancho was furious!

"It was a bum rap and I didn't intend to let them get away with it. A bunch of us 'Lady' pilots including Bobby Trout, Nancy Chaffee, Patty Wills, March Charles, Viola Neal, and me put on a protest air show in Washington D.C. to show our displeasure with the way they had treated Duncan. President Franklin Delano Roosevelt was so delighted with our show that he listened to us and pardoned Duncan. I always will believe that President Roosevelt saw some real trouble coming our way and he wanted to make damn sure we were on his side. He was a real man but his son, Elliott, who later commanded Muroc was a real horse's ass."

*　*　*

The valley of the Mojave where Pancho chose to settle was called the Antelope Valley because of the heavy population of antelope many years past. A natural lake on the east end of the desert provided water for the antelope and the vegetation of the mountain foothills gave them a good grazing area. Legend is that when the Southern Pacific Railroad connecting Los Angeles and Bakersfield was built that it separated the water hole and the grazing land and the antelope were afraid to cross the railroad tracks. Others said that hunters decimated the herd. Whatever the reason, by the time Pancho started her ranch the antelope were gone but the name lingered on.

The weather in the Antelope Valley was excellent for flying and a natural location for flying fields for training flight crews and evaluating airplane performance. As the war started in Europe and the war clouds started blowing toward America, it was obvious that we were painfully short in numbers of aircraft and crews to fly them, so the valley of the Antelope became a budding flight training center.

Pancho, with her excellent flying field and her pilot expertise, was chosen to operate a training school for civilian pilots. The Civilian Pilot Training (CPT) program served two purposes: for students who were entering into the Air Corps Aviation Cadet program it was a sounding board for an early evaluation of their ability to fly and an introduction to flight training; for others it provided flight training so that they could become a part of a nucleus of civilian pilots who would be used for training other pilots, ferrying airplanes all over the world, flying cargo for military logistic support, and flight testing. Kirk Kerkorian, a present-day multi-million-aire and former owner of MGM, learned to fly at Pancho's school. He worked as a stable-hand to pay for lessons and board.

In addition to the flight school, Pancho had a triple threat deal going with her hogs. She charged the military at the blossoming air base for collecting their garbage, fed the garbage to her pigs, and then sold the meat of the slaughtered pigs back to the mess hall at the base!

At the beginning of 1941, Pancho had it all together and her beautiful Rancho Oro Verde and CPT flying school were in great shape, a helluva lot more than her air corps neighbors at Muroc Army Air Field who were playing "catch-up" for a nation caught with no aerial reserves as a war threatened to explode around them.

9

The year 1942 was one of chaos. The United States had been caught unprepared for the war into which she had been drawn. Materiel and men suddenly were in short supply, and the frenzy of war embraced the nation in an unwanted hug. Men were being drafted, new military bases were being opened and the old bases were expanded. Muroc Army Air Field was suddenly a beehive of activity with P-38, B-24, and B-25 aircraft crew training and some secret-shrouded flight testing. Pancho's ranch grew along with the war and with Muroc.

From Muroc to Los Angeles was a tortuous one hundred plus miles of a single lane asphalt road through the mountains. Gasoline was rationed, cars at the base were few, military bus transportation was infrequent and inconvenient. Air base entertainment was limited to movies and drinking at the PX or one of the clubs. Those men who got to know Pancho started spending some of their idle time at her ranch and then they would bring their friends. It wasn't long until the ranch was an unofficial gathering place for off-duty airmen. Many of the visitors came just to escape the monotony of the base, some to talk with Pancho, and others to ride her horses. For want of any other name it was called a riding club.

"Now I don't care what anyone says, my club was a riding club. Horses and riders went out every hour and both officers and enlisted men were at ease relaxing around my place. It was against military regulations to be out of uniform at any time but the regulation said that for those men

76

engaged in sports activities being out of uniform was O.K. I convinced the brass that horseback riding was a sport the same as football and basketball and if men got out of uniform for those sports they could fucking well get out of uniform to participate in horseback riding at my club. After the usual stupid battle with the assholes who had regulations for brains, I finally won and both officers and enlisted men dressed in plaid shirts and khaki pants while they were at the club.

"Everyone was called by their first name. There was no rank distinction at the club and this promoted a great camaraderie among the men. Any man who carried the same familiarity back to the base was booted out of the club and any officer found pulling rank at the club was also booted out."

The club grew and it needed a name. Pancho tells of two incidents that combined to give the ranch riding club the unique name of "Happy Bottom Riding Club":

"I traded for a beautiful new easy-riding mare and after one of the lady guests rode her she remarked that the horse was so comfortable to ride that it made your bottom want to smile. Then Dr. Fred Reynolds, an eye surgeon at the base, put the name to the club. Any newcomer to the club after riding the first few times would have a butt so sore that he had to eat standing up. Old-timers had happy bottoms because they had learned to ride and toughened up. Dr. Reynolds proposed calling full-fledged members part of the 'Happy Bottom Riding Club' and the name caught on and stuck. There were people who always read a different meaning into the name of the club and they had some pretty nasty origins dreamed up in their small fucking minds but it was just as Dr. Reynolds had suggested—that plain and simple.

"The club was a big success. I was making money, the boys were having fun and everybody was happy. To add a little class I brought a few lovely girls from Hollywood to act as hostesses at the club. I brought them up for adornments for the club and to give the guys something to chase. Men love to chase girls and it seems that most of the fun is in the chase, so I gave them the girls to chase. If my guys wanted a different kind of action, they could have gone to Los Angeles and hired the most expensive of call girls or picked up some of the floozies who were always floating around the nearby towns. These guys were isolated in the middle of the desert and were happy to have the sweet smell of lovely female companionship.

"One day while I was in Hollywood taking care of some business I decided to give the boys a real treat. I brought three extra-lovely girls back to the ranch with me and they put on a spectacular show and dance routine. More than 400 of the boys were there that night and every man in the audience mentally disrobed each one of those girls. The girls were carried away with the enthusiasm of those men and rewarded them by doing a total strip tease right down to their lovely naked bodies. The desert rocked with the roar of the crowd as each piece of clothing was artistically removed. A beautiful show and a lot of fun for everybody. Not a goddamned thing wrong with it, either. Worse things go on every night in the puritan groups who call their shows 'fashion shows' and 'artistic dancing'. Hell, at least I was honest about it and called the show exactly what it was—a well-performed nude strip tease by three damned good-looking girls.

"After that there were more girls but they weren't strippers or tarts like some of the latter-day sainted sonsovbitches accused me of having. They were beauties and acted as hostesses. I would go down to Los Angeles and while staying in the Beverly Hills Hotel would advertise for girls who were interested in working at the ranch. Hollywood was full of young, beautiful girls who were looking for that "big break" but were finding it to be very elusive. They were working at any kind of job they could get and were always reading the want ads so I got a good response to my ads and always first class girls. I picked out their clothes to complement the best features of the individual girl and when they got dressed up there were some real knockouts. You know, if you dress and make up an average-looking girl you can do wonders for her and if you have a good-looking one you can come up with something sensational.

"Proper lighting is another trick to making a girl look good, and I had learned all about that from my days of working in the movies. To hear some people tell about it, all that I had for lighting was a naked 100-watt light bulb but that's a lot of bullshit. I had one girl that wouldn't attract any attention at all in daylight, but when I draped her in a filmy turquoise thing, fixed her hair, dangled some glittery earrings from her ears, and put her under a soft light, every man on the reservation was captivated.

"Another misconception was that these girls were empty-headed dummies with good bodies. When I hired them, I picked the ones who were not only good-looking but who could carry on a discussion that reached beyond all of the normal Hollywood bullshit. Some of these girls were honor students and when they were selected as Miss Scranton or something they rushed to Hollywood to become overnight movie stars. Many of these girls were real smart kids who just got too much stardust in their eyes.

"Lots of the boys at the base were just kids and not too far removed from their farm homes in Iowa or South Carolina. Sure, they liked to chase my girls, but they also wanted someone other than another soldier to talk with. There were kids who fell in love with each other at the club and even a couple of marriages took place.

"For the sake of protecting the girls, I had them all use the last name of Smith and to choose the name of a month, day of the week, or state for a first name. So we had names like January Smith, Nevada Smith, and Tuesday Smith. Names like these added a bit of glamour and mystique to the girls and the guys loved it.

"We were in the middle of a war and whether we liked to admit it or not, our boys were getting killed in it. Christ, there's no telling how many of them were killed just in flight training here at Muroc. There was nothing to do at the base, goddamned stuffed-shirt brass wouldn't let them hitch-hike to Los Angeles or Vegas, so I made a place for them to have a little fun and relaxation. Some people can never see the good in anything, then drift through life drowned in their own fucking smugness and criticize everybody else. Narrow minded bastards think that the only reason a boy scout helps an old lady across the street is to steal her purse. Same thing with my ranch, all the do-gooders telling each other that a place with good-looking girls couldn't be anything but a whorehouse. Truth was that my girls behaved a helluva lot better than some of them in these alleged chaste convents.

"I had heard a lot of these nasty accusations and had even put a sign up over the bar to explain to some of these tunnel-vision assholes that the club was a drink and dance club and not a love-for-sale dive:

WE ARE NOT RESPONSIBLE FOR THE BUSTLING AND HUSTLING THAT MAY GO ON HERE. LOTS OF PEOPLE BUSTLE AND SOME HUSTLE, BUT THAT'S THEIR BUSINESS AND A VERY OLD ONE.

"My girls were just the sugar to catch the boys. What kind of arrangements or what they did after hours was their own business. These boys were big enough to get their asses shot down so surely they were big enough to handle girls. There were some pretty strict rules about the girls not drinking hard stuff and dating men during working hours. But just like every other goddamned rule in the world, someone broke it every now and then."

Bill Bridgeman, a tall, balding ex-Navy pilot was flying for NACA (now NASA) in the X series research program and in concert with Jacqueline Hazard wrote a book titled *The Lonely Sky*, telling of his flight experiences at Muroc. He described Pancho's club or Fly-Inn as "Furnished with rickety tables, dirty glasses, and looking as if the door had been left open and the desert had blown in." He went on to add that it was "Run by an extremely ugly old woman . . ." and so forth. When Pancho read that particular passage, she frowned a bit and then her eyes lit up with that special sparkle that belonged to her alone.

"Ugly, I'll accept, but extremely ugly is taking it too far. I'll get that sonofabitch when I write my book. Problem with

Bill was that he was chasing one of my girls and having trouble catching her. He asked me to give him a little help or put in a good word for him, so to speak. I told him that he was a big grown man and that he shouldn't have to have any help in his girl chasing. He really got pissed off and has been sorta mad at me ever since. Bill is a damned good pilot and after I take my pound of flesh for his smart ass remarks we'll have a few belly laughs and everything will be O.K."*

Wednesday night was a special dance night at the Happy Bottom Riding Club and as many as 400 men from the base showed up to join the revelry. During the lull of silence between the takeoffs of the airplanes at the base, the roar of delight from Pancho's echoed across the lonely desert. In general, they raised hell and enjoyed every moment of it. Why not? These were men and boys whose future was filled with a trip to the rigors and unknowns of war. They had been ordered from the familiar and comfortable surroundings of their homes, abused by the sadistic rituals of training, and stuck in the middle of the Mojave Desert as a last look at the good life. The club was a breath of fresh air from the suffocating routines of constant day and night flight training. It was an escape valve that kept them from blowing up emotionally. It was one of the last inns along their pathway to a new life of death and destruction. Some of the men were there at the club because they thoroughly enjoyed it, others because there was nothing else to do, and still others because they felt it necessary to follow the habits of their peers.

As some of the "holier-than-thou" detractors screamed that it was an immoral place, perhaps it was by their narrow and small-minded evaluations. Assuming that the worst of these accusations was true, how could anyone in his right mind condemn it when just a short walk away men were being trained to kill and destroy. Suppose the girls did shack up with the lonely flyers. Suppose they did share their love with them and suppose they "charged" them for it. What the hell? The blue-noses thought that it was great for the

---

*Bill Bridgeman was killed in a flying accident in 1969.

men to be taught to kill, an odious thing that was against all of their natural instincts. It was fine that they be housed in tents filled with blowing sand, lizards, sidewinders, and scorpions, and it was magnificent when they swept the desert with machine gun fire and bombs.

The alternatives to going to Pancho's club were few and generally lousy. Base clubs were supervised by some sticky officer who ran a tight ship to gain approval from his superiors and there was never anyone in the clubs except other guys as lonely and bored as the guy next to him. There was the beer drinking possibility at the Post Exchange where they could drink themselves to some degree of insensibility while they snapped their fingers to Johnny Mercer's "G.I. Jive" as it blared over and over from the jukebox. Every now and then some insensitive bastard would play "I'll Walk Alone" or something equally as sentimental and some of the guys would sit in the darkness on the rough PX steps so their buddies wouldn't see the tears of loneliness and frustration in their eyes.

Why not go to Pancho's? Here there was happy music and camaraderie. Here there was no rank and no signs of authority. This was a million miles away from a goddamned war and from the outside latrines where a man couldn't even take a piss in private. Here, if you were lucky, you might get to share a real room with a pretty, soft, sweet-smelling girl. You could escape from the fucked-up realities of tough training for a man-killing task. You could burrow your head into the soft shoulder of a lovely girl and for that moment feel safe and comfortable. For those magic moments you were not one of a million other look-alike G.I.s and you didn't have to say "Yes, sir" to some ass who was your intellectual superior because he'd taken R.O.T.C. (Reserve Officer Training Corps) in school. For awhile, you were human again and home free.

The availability of the girls to dance with was a big plus in the lives of the guys. The jukebox could play its sentimental "I'll Get By" and rather than sit on the PX steps and cry or lie on your bunk and stare at emptiness, you were content and comfortable because you were reassured that real girls did exist and for the moment you had one. The intoxication of perfume and the soft yielding body was a balm to cure the hurts of the day. It was great for a blue-haired lady to give you a box of fried chicken at a troop train whistle stop but it was a helluva lot better to have a platinum blonde hold you close as she softly hummed a love song to you. You take the U.S.O. Buster, I'll take Pancho's.

Pancho didn't confine her activities to just providing a place for the fly boys to let off a bit of steam for she had a sentimental streak that wouldn't stay camouflaged. One night at the club a young lieutenant was describing a foreign-made roadster he had seen for sale in Los Angeles. Most beautiful car he had ever seen and more expensive than he had ever imagined. Pancho looked at the boy-like man pilot and the thought that he would be in combat in a few weeks and maybe back home in a box in a few more came to her mind. She got the dealer's name, called him, and asked that he meet her at his showroom and then announced that she was going to Los Angeles to buy a car. Everyone in the club who had a car decided to go along and there in the middle of a black night, a cavalcade of cars driven by hot-rock pilots headed for Los Angeles.

The highway from Pancho's to Los Angeles was a narrow asphalt strip that wound its way through the San Bernardino mountains and provided little in the nature of conveniences along the way. It took a couple of hours and change for the happy band of warriors to get to the car dealer's but they made it in one piece and she bought the snappy little roadster for the lieutenant. As they headed back toward Muroc through the San Fernando Valley, a California sheriff stopped them and put them all under arrest for an assorted number of charges. They were all highly suspected of being escapees from some sort of mental confinement center. Sheriff Biscailuz, the chief sheriff of Los Angeles County, had made Pancho an honorary deputy and had given her a miniature golden badge. Pancho flashed this bit of authority to the arresting officer and suggested that he call his boss for some advice before he had her caravan hauled off to jail.

Sheriff Biscailuz advised the officer to round up a couple more motorcycle officers and for them to escort Pancho's circus to Muroc. Somewhere around dawn an eerie parade of cars led and followed by police officers with the lights on their motorcycles flashing, rolled into the parking lot of the Happy Bottom Riding Club. A very happy young lieutenant driving a British green roadster with a right-hand drive led the entourage. A beaming Pancho was his co-pilot.

In its day, Pancho's club was the most complete hotel in the Antelope Valley, featuring air-conditioned rooms with private baths, cocktail lounge, excellent food at all hours, rodeo grounds, hay rides, swimming pool and 24-hour airport service.

Below: **Mac and Pancho check over plans for one of their rodeos.**

Around 1949 to 1950 Pancho and the VFW often held rodeos at Pancho's Antelope Valley ranch.

Capt. Charles E. Yeager, the first man to fly faster than the speed of sound in the X-1 shown above, learned to ride and rope at Pancho's. He found riding to be a good sport for a test pilot.

Above: **A wagon from the Happy Bottom Club meeting a plane at the Barnes Airport.** Below: Frank Tallman and Paul Mantz, two of movielands foremost stunt and movie pilots had a small aerial museum in Ontario, California. There, in a shambles, was Pancho's old Mystery S. One afternoon Pancho, Paul and the author were having lunch at the Edwards AFB club when Pancho asked if she could have her airplane back so her son Billy could restore it to flying condition. Paul told her that she could have it any time she sent a truck to pick it up. None of them, having an abundance of money, Tate conned a General Dynamics truck driver to pick up the aircraft remains anytime he was in the area. Before they got the airplane picked up Paul Mantz was killed in an airplane during the filming of the movie, "The Flight of the Phoenix." Shortly after the airplanes in the museum were sold at auction. This photo shows Pancho and her son Billy after they "won" the auction bid of $4,300. Pancho wanted the airplane restored so that she could fly it again but Billy had some misgivings about this idea and the airplane was not restored during Pancho's lifetime.

Above: **Pancho Barnes, General Albert Boyd, Susan Oliver and Fish Salmon. Each of these made individual contributions to the advancement of aviation and to its history. Pancho set speed records, General Boyd held world speed records and later commanded the fledgling flight test center and Fish was a premier test pilot for Lockheed. Susan Oliver is the only woman to fly solo to Russia and is the only surviving member of the group.** Below: **Author, Ted Tate, and famed racing pilot Roscoe Turner during a familiarization look at the F-111 cockpit. Pancho and Roscoe were air race competitors.**

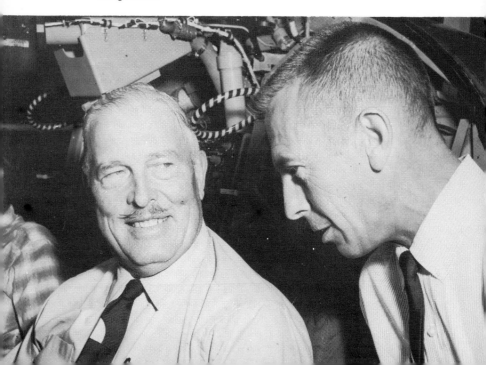

Above: **Bill Dana, NASA test pilot, presenting Pancho with a placque autographed by all who flew the X-15, the space pioneering bullet that Pete Knight flew at a speed in excess of 4500 mph. Among the signatures on the placque is that of Neil Armstrong, the first man to walk on the moon. From Pancho's wing-walking days to Armstrong's moon walk doesn't represent a lot of calendar time but a whale of a bunch of progress in flying.** Below: **A meeting of historic eras. Buzz Aldrin, who walked on the moon with Neil Armstrong and Jimmy Doolittle whose aviation racing, engineering and wartime pursuits would fill several books. General Doolittle was the first pilot to make a "blind" instrument landing. He led the daring first aerial raid on Tokyo in WWII and later commanded the Eighth Air Force in England. Photo taken at a party honoring Pancho.**

Above: **Ted Tate presenting General Doolittle with a gold plated No. 1 membership placque to the Happy Bottom Riding Club.** Below: **Pancho and Boots Le Boutellier.** Boots, at the time of this photo was the only surviving American pilot who witnessed the shooting down of the Red Baron.

Above: **Author, Ted Tate at a reunion with Pancho Barnes. Ted spent 37 years in the aviation business as mechanic, engineer, pilot, gunner, navigator, bombardier. He retired from the U.S. Air Force Reserve after non-spectacular service [his description] in three major conflicts. Member of Silver Wings, Mach II Club and the Adventurers Club, Ted now lives in Zihuatanejo, Mexico with his only flying activities being those experienced in once-in-awhile commercial flights to far away places with strange sounding names, such as Los Angeles.**

William E. "Bill" Barnes, Pancho's son, became an accomplished pilot in his own right. He held a commercial license as a pilot and also an aircraft engine mechanic's license. He managed the Barnes' Airport. Bill loved hunting and fishing and was, like his mother, an excellent horseman. At one time he trained and worked horses in motion pictures.

Above: **Pancho's son Billy followed a flying career and was ultimately killed in this crash of a P-51 Mustang which he was flying for an air show at Edwards AFB only a few miles from the site of the happy Bottom Riding Club.**

The club and the civilian pilot training program endured the war years and provided the wild blue yonder guys with a piece of life as necessary to their existence as the sandy chow they got at the base. God alone or perhaps some dusty record keeper knows how many heroes were spawned at the club and pilot school. There were hundreds of pictures of students and graduates strung all over the walls of the club, some of guys gone on to greater glories as generals and such and some just plain gone on to greater glory—wherever that might be.

I don't know how anyone else remembers it, but I feel that there is nothing more representative of the spirit that sparked the United States to win the "big" war or the Korean fiasco than a bunch of well-oiled airmen clustered around someone playing a rinky-tink piano. It was that way at Pancho's. Who the hell cared if a few of the keys stuck, no one could play the piano very well anyway—except for January Smith, a lady as lovely as the classical symphonies she could coax from that old piano. Perhaps I'm a nostalgia buff or a war lover or a hero worshipper or insane. But whenever I wander about the old ranch site I can still hear the harmony or cacophony of a group with voices like wounded cats and castrated bull dogs giving it all they had. "Don't Sit Under the Apple Tree," "Smoke Gets in Your Eyes," "Lili Marlene," "Down by the Old Mill Stream," "Goodnight Sweetheart," "On a Wing and a Prayer," "I Get Along Without You Very Well," "Harbor Lights," "I Wanted Wings Til I Got the Goddamned Things," "When

You're a Long Long Way From Home." The closing hymn was always the raunchiest, the loudest, the most off-key, the favorite, the best—"We live in fame or go down in flame, nothing can stop the Army Air Corps. Goodnight ladies, goodnight." The marines had a flag at Iwo Jima, the Air Corps had a piano.

As the era of ill-fitting khakis, olive drab woolens, classy pinks and greens closed out and a new one was waiting in the wings, the Happy Bottom Riding Club made the transition with a flair. The mission of the base changed and the profiles of the buildings were different but the desert silhouette with its sentinels of grotesque joshua trees remained king of the hill. The faces changed but not the character behind those faces. Whoever or whatever they were, they were still the aerial warriors, and the crystal-clear blue sky above the Mojave was their arena. These guys had fought and won the battle for survival and now were the pioneers of progress, often burdened with far more problems and threats of death than had been their fare in combat. Pancho, April, January, and all of the other Smith girls were the refuge from reality. There were housing and wives and families and officers clubs and movies and swimming pools and social clubs and beer bars on the base but there wasn't the freedom to sing some ball-bustin' "There are no Fighter Pilots Down in Hell" classic while January Smith tickled the black and whites and whetted your appetite for the sweetness of life. Pancho, God bless you and April and January and all of those soft lovely sweet-smelling ladies who didn't get all riled up if you slipped up and used a few barracks verbs and adjectives.

The club, as Pancho maintained, was a riding club and many of the wives and children of the fliers joined them for horseback riding. One of the most colorful twosomes was an outstanding fighter-pilot hero, Charles E "Chuck" Yeager and his beautiful wife Glennis. Hundreds of stories have been written about Chuck, his wartime heroics, his supreme test flights, and his delightful low-key personality. Whenever God made Chuck he was either extra pleased or extra disappointed with the result because He only made one like him and must have forgotten the formula.

Chuck was selected or volunteered or bribed his way into the pilot's seat of the rocket-powered X-1 in its mission to fly faster than the speed of sound. Chuck got the job after the Bell Company X-1 project Pilot asked for a bonus about equal to a cushy movie star's weekly pay—in the neighborhood of $150,000. With the change in pilots, the fee went down dramatically to about $300 a month, a few extra bucks for the joy of flying and a pittance for family sustenance. Maybe a total of around $500 a month or for about $17 a day rather than the 150 grand. The flight was only good for about ten minutes so when the economics were sifted to that level he made a bit over 35 cents for the flight—probably the best bargain the USA government ever got or will ever get again.

A couple of days before the scheduled supersonic try in the X-1, Chuck and Glennis had gone for a desert horseback ride and Chuck had kept going after his horse did a sudden deceleration at a closed gate. Chuck hit the fence, busted a couple of ribs, and created a lot of pain for himself. Flight surgeons were created to keep flight crews healthy and physically happy but they also had a tendency to "ground" people when they found them suffering from minor aggravations such as bad hearts and broken ribs. To avoid these unpleasant grounding scenes with the doctors, flight crew members would resort to self-healing, witch doctors, or "bite the bullet" and endure procedures. I once had some of the guys in the barracks pour some booze over a boil under my armpit, slit it open with a flame-sterilized Gillette razor blade, force out the accumulated poisons with their cigarette stained fingers, and then anoint the wound with some iodine we had stolen from an aircraft first-aid kit—all to keep from facing the "grounding" for a few days. Chuck Yeager was much smarter—he went to a civilian doctor in a nearby town. The doctor taped the ribs, told him to minimize the use of his right arm, and that he'd be O.K. in a couple of weeks. Chuck could fly the X-1 O.K. with the restricted right arm but he couldn't actuate the canopy lock lever without really hurting so Jackie Ridley, one of the project engineers, gave Yeager a piece of broomstick to use to push the canopy lock-lever closed. With that arrangement, a $2-an-hour pilot and a goddamned broomstick, the X-1 flew to Mach 1.05, beyond the speed of sound and the new frontier of space was penetrated.

The news of Chuck Yeager's heroic and historic flight was not formally released until eight months after the flight but when the X-1 had busted the sound barrier the shock wave boomed all over the desert and all of the troops at Pancho's knew what had happened. There was a helluva celebration at the club that night but it was somewhat like other celebrations because no one was allowed to say what they were celebrating. Pancho saw a chink in the Air Force's claim to the first supersonic flight so she confided in her good friend Chuck Yeager.

"I know we got there first, but I hear a few rumblings about the fucking navy thinking that it wasn't a big deal to go supersonic after being dropped from another airplane. They're planning to fly something off of the lake and then accelerate it to Mach 1 or better and lay claim to being the first *airplane* to go supersonic. Those assholes are saying that you can *drop* a rock with a firecracker tied to it and it'll go supersonic. They're full of shit as a Christmas goose but they'll do what they're planning and make a big fucking deal of it.

"We're going to outsmart those peckerwoods at their own game. You're going to Washington and hang around outside of Secretary of the Air Force Stuart Symington's office and when he asks how you are, you're gonna tell him not worth a shit because of what the fucking navy has up their sleeve. He's gonna be real interested and you're gonna tell him that with his direction and a few extra bucks that you and Ridley and a couple of other smart cookies around here can rig up something to take off from the lake and go Mach 1 or better. Symington's gonna give the O.K. and we're gonna do just what we said."

Things worked out like she said. There was some quick "back of an envelope" engineering worked out, the aircraft was modified, and on January 5, 1959, Charles E. Yeager took off from Rogers Dry Lake Bed and accelerated to supersonic speeds.

Pancho had a love and respect for Chuck Yeager that can only be understood by those who have shared similar relationships. He was a man who did all of those things with an airplane that she admired and regardless of the fame he achieved, remained the same unaffected friend. She was often critical of the news media because she felt that Chuck had never been given the worldwide recognition that he deserved.

"Chuck was the first pilot to crack the sound barrier and don't let anyone try to tell you any different. There are all kinds of stories about yahoos diving F-86s to supersonic speed but that's a lot of bullshit. Chuck did it first and he *piloted* the airplane to make his record. Any bitch dog or monkey can be sent around the world in a capsule and can push buttons on a signal—Pavlov proved that a long time ago. Chuck did his flight using his own brain and pilot know-how. Most of these news people don't know a hero from a drugged monkey."

At one time there were as many as 9000 "card-carrying" members of the Happy Bottom Riding Club and among them were movie luminaries, politicians, and high-ranking military officers. Pancho threatened to write a book about the activities of some of the members but decided that she could probably make a fortune by charging each of the real-life characters $100 for not putting them in the book.

Some of the club members often made outrageous requests for accommodations and luxurious extras. Pancho usually complied in kind and with a flair.

"A couple of two-star generals called me from Wright-Pat in Dayton and said that they would be at Muroc in a couple of days. They asked that I provide them with bed, board, booze, and broads. What the hell did they really want? They explained that they wanted the best guest rooms, the finest steak, some good Scotch that wasn't one of my Mexican refills and a couple of willing girls who were first-class "eating stuff." Always being one to do things up movie style, I decided to give these peckerheads a show.

"I had two big aluminum serving trays made and had the baker in town make up two giant loaves of bread. The brass arrived, I gave them the fanciest rooms, served them big steak dinners with good booze and told them the girls would join them in their rooms later. We made sandwiches from the two loaves of bread with a nude, lovely girl between the two huge slices of bread. A couple of the boys acted as waiters and delivered the 'sandwiches' to the generals' rooms. Everybody was delighted but there were some pictures taken that night that gave me a bit of trouble a few years later.

"And speaking of booze, I used to buy a little Mexican stuff that somehow or another got delivered to me without taxes being paid. One evening when a load was being delivered I got word that some of the officers at Muroc were bringing some civilian Federal boys over that same evening. The truckload of booze got there while the Feds were being entertained so Ira Reed and I dug a big hole out in the desert with a tractor and buried the whole shipment. Later that night one of those sudden gulley-washer desert rains damn near washed us away and kinda' rearranged some of the desert landmarks.

"The next day Ira and some of the boys searched for hours and they never did find that buried booze. Far as I know, it's still out there somewhere like some of the other gold mines that have been lost and no one can find them. Ira and some of his crazy Hollywood flying buddies used to make special trips up here just to search the desert but they never found the buried booze."

There was a neat little rodeo arena on the ranch and Pancho staged rodeos and barbecues for her guests that became legends. People would fly in to her little airstrip from all over the U.S. and Mexico to attend these events. To spice up the rodeo, Pancho had specialty acts and outstanding among them was Lady Godiva. This lady was a bit on the pudgy size and was more in place on a Goya painting but she was a supremely talented trick rider and put on a real performance. Maybe it was the fact that Lady Godiva wore only a flesh-colored body stocking and appeared to be doing her tricks in the nude that made her so popular. Souvenir programs for the Lady Godiva act were instant collector's items and I wouldn't take anything for the one that I have hidden away among my treasures.

After Chuck Yeager's blast to supersonic glory, other pilots in other exotic airborne vehicles joined him in "Blowin' and Goin' " supersonic. It was only natural that a fraternity of these real pioneers of space and speed be named the Blow and Go Club. The suit and tie set may put people like Henry Kissinger on their Hall of Fame slates but for me it should be the Blow and Go guys. Christ, what a line-up! Chuck Yeager, Joe Walker, Bill Bridgeman, Jack McKay, Pete Everest, Kit Murray, Mel Apt, and Ivan Kinchelde. These guys did things, they made things happen, and celebrated at Pancho's while she told them they really didn't know a fucking thing about flying until they had flown a real airplane powered by an OX-5!

While all of the shenanigans of fighting the war, transitioning to other pursuits, and the flights to the edge of space were going on, Pancho was creating her own supersonic whirlwinds.

Those people in government who are in charge of naming streets and parks and holidays and other tasks that justify their megabucks salaries changed Muroc Dry Lake to Rogers Dry Lake and Muroc Air Force Base to Edwards AFB. The change to Rogers, Pancho tolerated but to change Muroc Base to Edwards really hacked her. Although the new name was chosen as a tribute to test pilot Glenn Edwards who was killed in the crash of the Northrop Y15-49 "Flying Wing" at Muroc, Pancho was riled.

"God damn it, Muroc has a history that reaches back to 1934 with those raggedy-assed kids dropping their wallowing bombs all over the fucking desert to Chuck Yeager becoming history's first supersonic pilot. Not only that, but the first Air Force jet, the P-59, was flown here and it's part of our history.

"They aren't about to change the names of battlegrounds like Valley Forge so why change Muroc? It's a battleground with a particular history all of its own. Who knows but that more flight crews burned in their airplanes here than died in battle at Valley Forge? Muroc is sacred ground and let's by God keep it that way."

Pancho lost that battle just as she lost two more tries. In the matrimonial arena, she finally divorced the Reverend Barnes in 1942 and subsequently married a flight student named Nichols in 1942 and divorced him in 1944. After Nichols she married a Persian named Don Shalita and he lasted until around 1951. She had no children by any of these marriages so her family was just herself and her son, "Billy Barnes."

She fought all sorts of court battles with the Air Force and really had a salty fight when her Happy Bottom Riding Club was declared off-limits to all military personnel. She won this one but it was only a prelude to the big war that was yet to come.

More beautiful girls were imported from Hollywood to be playmates for the post-war supersonic airmen. More people were at the base and more people were at the club. It grew until it was a Mexican-like hacienda. There was a beautiful terrace and fountain, swimming pool, private rooms for the girls, dining room, bar, dance floor, guest rooms, and a suite of special rooms. It has been described as everything from baroque to brkkk. Whatever it was, it was a magnet for off-duty airmen and a place where a man could temporarily forget the flameouts, control oscillations, equipment malfunctions, onboard fires, and lost comrades of the test flying business only a stone's throw away.

It was also becoming a pain in the ass to Air Force brass.

11

On June 30, 1952, the first real "jet set" and the Blow and Go guys assembled at Pancho's for her marriage to Eugene S. "Mac" McKendry, a veteran combat pilot and navigator. It was Pancho's fourth and last marriage and a real "ball-buster."

More than 1500 people assembled at the Happy Bottom Riding Club and while the blast of the jets and rockets from Edwards AFB was stilled for the day, the roar from Pancho's was thunderous enough to make the sidewinders seek refuge. The guest list was a "Who's Who" of the airplane and space test business with a few of Hollywood's glittering stars thrown in for added glamour.

With her usual flair, Pancho engineered a wedding party that surely made old Bacchus sit back and giggle with glee.

"I brought an ice sculptor from Hollywood who carved out figures inside blocks of ice and when the ice blocks were filled with red wine the figures came alive. The day was hot as hell but the crowd I had, the wine didn't last long enough for the ice to melt. We roasted pigs, chickens and turkeys, baked fish and boiled lobster. There was a ton of salads of all kinds, deviled eggs by the hundreds and enough dinner rolls to feed the entire base for a week.

"It was a real fancy affair with everything done with class. The men all wore suits and ties and the women wore beautiful dinner dresses. For the first time in God knows how long I put on a dress and high heeled shoes and felt downright foolish in such a rig. Guess we have to make some concessions to so-called social graces."

General Albert Boyd, the Commanding Officer of
Edwards Air Force Base, gave the bride away and Chuck
Yeager was best man. General Boyd was one of the Air
Force generals who impressed Pancho.

"Al was a real commander of men. He flew everything the
goddamned designers came up with and flew it better than
anyone else. He was a gentleman with style. I loved that
man. When I married McKendry, Al was in Dayton and set
up a record speed run of some kind to get to Edwards for the
wedding. When he got here, he rolled that beautiful shiny
B-47 over the ranch, landed and got to the club looking like
he'd just stepped out of a board meeting of some big
company. Most of the cardboard generals weren't fit to kiss
the boots of men like Al Boyd."

It was my privilege to fly with General Boyd on several
test flights and I fully agreed with Pancho. General Boyd
told me to call him Al but he was a man of such imposing
dignity and bearing that I could never address him in any
manner other than General Boyd. When I told him that for
me to call him Al would be like taking the Lord's name in
church, he was astounded. We had a few disagreements
during a couple of flights and I had been a bit vociferous in
stating my opinions so General Boyd could not understand
my reluctance to be more familiar on the ground.

Before some of the more restrictive rules came into being,
General Albert Boyd was the only man in the Air Force who
was "current" or "checked out" to fly any aircraft in the Air
Force inventory. To see and to be with this man in his
carefully chosen suit and Countess Mara tie made it difficult
to believe that he was one of the "hottest" pilots in the
business. He held the world's speed record of 624 MPH until
1948. Lloyd Nolan played a part in the movie *Toward the
Unknown* that was a thin representation of General Boyd
when he was commander of the Flight Test Center.

With Lieutenant Colonel Chuck Yeager and General
Albert Boyd as her "family", Pancho had the best. As they
stood before Judge J.G. Sherrill for the marriage ceremony,
twenty-two years of aviation progress was represented.
Pancho had set the woman's airplane speed record of 196

MPH in 1930 and both Chuck Yeager and Al Boyd were pilots of supersonic vehicles. Chuck and Al were both highly decorated combat pilots and were supreme test pilots. In that little group of three standing before Judge Sherrill was one hell of a lot of aviation history and some of the outstanding heroes who had made it.

Pancho was inordinately proud of a vein of American Indian that she claimed as part of her ancestry and for her wedding to Mac she had an Indian ceremony in addition to the legal pale-face performance. A chief of the Blackfoot tribe, Chief Lucky, brought fifty of his tribe to the Happy Bottom Club and performed a colorful ritualistic marriage ceremony that seemed to go on for hours.

It would have been unkind to leave the "in-residence" Smith girls out of the wedding festivities so Pancho let them stage a sort of nude water ballet in the swimming pool. For the guests, their cups runneth over and for Pancho and Mac they were off and running to make the Happy Bottom Riding Club's pace equal that of the rapidly growing Edwards Air Force Base, the U.S. Air Force's Flight Test Center.

12

Edwards Air Force Base is one of the largest in the world and encompasses over 300,000 acres. It has a natural 16-mile dry lake bed runway and a 15,000 foot concrete landing strip. The greatest pilots and astronauts in the world have touched down on the Edwards' pad and the dry lake bed has saved many of their butts whenever their machines suffered brake failure or other serious malfunctions. Thanks to the availability of the lake bed they lived to touch down another day. Pancho's land is now an unused part of this giant military reservation. It didn't come easy.

Early in 1953 the U.S. government filed a condemnation suit to get Pancho's land. The alleged reason was so that the runway could be extended to accommodate the new and future generations of jets and rockets.

"Bullshit. They acted like they wanted to build a runway from the base all the way to the fucking ocean. Those bluenoses just wanted my club out of there; wanted more land to add to their fucking empire and were not above using any means or methods to get their own way.

"Ever since 1947 those peckerheads had been giving me a hard time and planting the idea that the club was just a big cover-up for a whorehouse. I shoulda' sued those ol' bastards every day for the six or seven years that they hard-assed me.

"Those goddamned dummies used such asinine logic as 'What else could a club with a name like Happy Bottom be but a whorehouse?' If I'd wanted to run a whorehouse for those horny bastards it would have been a real one—one that

96

looked like a whorehouse and had red velvet class. Bunch of goddamned pissants who were giving me all of the trouble probably never had the guts to go into a real live whorehouse and didn't have the faintest fucking idea of what they were talking about.''

In 1952 Pancho's old buddy, General Al Boyd, was succeeded as commander of the Edwards Flight Test Center by General J. Stanley Holtoner and it was he and Pancho who went to the center of the arena to lock horns.

"Those pissants had tried every way in the world to discredit me and to have my butt kicked out and they even resorted to some physical rough stuff. A young lieutenant wrote a letter to his commanding officer and told him that he had hired a girl at the Happy Bottom Club and that started a whole chain of ugly circumstances. The general gave the letter to the FBI and instead of chasing bad guys these sonsuvbitches came out to investigate my club. They rounded up all of my girls and tried to get them to admit that they were call girls. They brought up a whole portfolio of pictures of Los Angeles and Hollywood call girls and asked my girls if they knew any of the girls in the photos. Of course they didn't know any of them. I told the FBI that if I was really running a whorehouse that they could have found it out in a couple of days instead of the fourteen weeks it took them to find out not a goddamned thing.

"While all of the FBI crap was going on someone fired eight shots at me but the closest they came to hitting me was one bullet in my car. I took the bullet to a Judge, Judge Carter, and told him what had happened. He always helped me out and he must have tipped somebody because that ended the target practice.''

Pancho fired the first real salvo in what was to become the "War of the Mojave" when she filed a $1,483,000 suit against General Holtoner because it had to be filed against an individual and not against the government. She acted as her own attorney and started things by letting the court know that she had a pedigree and that they weren't dealing with a lightweight.

"Plaintiff's grandfather, T.S.C. Lowe organized the first military aerial war unit in the world which is now the United States Air Force, and he was its first commander-in-chief.

"Plaintiff was reared in Pasadena society when it was still within its limits of 400 so she has been greatly chagrined by the fact that on or about August 1947 the commanding officer of the air base at Muroc, one Colonel Signa Gilky, put her entire ranch, including club, cocktail bar, restaurant, etc., off limits to military personnel.

"This action was in retaliation for a phone call plaintiff allegedly made to the Pentagon to complain of soldier brawlers who were tearing up the place.

"Plaintiff further charges that Colonel Gilky caused and/or failed to correct the broadcast impression that the reason for the ranch being put out of bounds was that it was a whorehouse.

"As a result of the actions of Colonel Gilky, great hordes of disreputable characters descended upon the ranch demanding to pay for women for sex privileges and scarcely a day elapsed that men have not come in their search to buy flesh.

"Plaintiff further charges that the ill-reputation created by Colonel Gilky for plaintiff has now traveled to the ends of the earth."

Pancho followed this suit up with another one for $1,253,546.29. She had good reasons for coming up with these strange "unrounded" numbers and using this same logic she later sued the Bank of America for 1/10th of 1 percent of their total wealth—a pittance at first glance but a potful when computed.

For the second suit Pancho charged the Air Force with damages resulting from "humiliation, insults, and ostracism brought about by inferences, implications, and impressions that her ranch was a whorehouse—all without one iota of cause."

In order to get General Holtoner into court it was necessary for him to be served a summons so he insulated himself from any possible process server and was as protected as a dictator. Legend is that Pancho paid a civil service worker $10,000 to deliver the summons. The story goes that the worker knocked on the general's locked office door, announced that some work needed to be done and slipped the summons to Holtoner when he was admitted. The worker was fired but was later reinstated and General Holtoner had been "summonsed."

The property condemnation case against Pancho and her inverse-condemnation suits really had nothing to do with whether the Happy Bottom Riding Club was a whorehouse or not but Pancho attacked it from that angle.

"Back in 1941 the government could have legally taken my property through proper means and with just compensation, and maybe I would have squealed like a stuck hog but that would have been about all. Or they could have appraised it at a decent price and taken it at such time in the future when they really needed it. Incidentally, twenty years later they still haven't needed it!

"Instead of that, these assholes dreamed up their whorehouse charge and figured they could run me off without a fight. I never ran away from a fight in my life and I'm sure as shit not running from these peckerwoods."

Pancho charged that General Holtoner had warned her that if she didn't get out someone might "accidentally" drop a napalm bomb on her ranch. She followed up that charge with a $300,000 suit against Holtoner for his alleged threat. While all of this was being channeled through the courts, the Happy Bottom Riding Club, with all of Pancho's treasures and the hallowed halls of the Blow and Go gang, burned to the ground. Pancho was heartbroken and furious. She knew that it had been set by an arsonist but couldn't prove it.

What the bluenoses couldn't accomplish, a set fire did exceedingly well.

It was a cold desert November of 1953, twenty years from the day when Pancho had forsaken the social whirl of Pasadena for the grubby life of a desert hog rancher.

13

The court battles between the tiny, tough pilot/hog rancher and the Air Force went on for a couple of years. Pancho, as her own attorney, proved that the "lawyer who defends himself has a fool for a client" was false and of bad judgment.

In the later years after the battlefield had cleared, tempers had cooled, and the harshness of the court encounters had mellowed with time, Pancho was still pissed off about the whole scene. For endless hours I would sit with her in the Desert Dust Wagon Wheel Cafe and bar or hunkered in the desert sand or on a corral rail and listen to her accounts of the legal fights with the "pissants."

She loved to roar across the desert with me in my top-off T-Bird and let the sweet winds blow through her hair. I would enter a narrow curve too fast, skid around a bit, grind up a bit of dirt from the road shoulder, and then dig out on the straightaway.

"You don't come close enough to bustin' your ass in those stupid airplanes with funny wings (F-111) but you've got to drive like a fucking maniac. I've had horses that use better judgment than you. You should have been in court with me, we'd really have torn them a new asshole. Did I ever tell you . . . ?

"When it looked like those harassing sonsuvbitches were going to beat me out of the ranch at their price and brand me as a whorehouse madam at the same time, I surprised them all. I rounded up twenty or thirty highly respected witnesses and they put Judge Campbell Beaumont and his troops straight.

"Walt Williams, one of your buddies who put Glenn around the world, told them that the club was just like I said and maybe some hanky-panky went on there but it was just normal boy-girl stuff that went on between any good-looking waitress and an admiring customer.

"The judge looked at lurid pictures taken at the club and presented as evidence, then ruled them inadmissible because he couldn't tell whether the girls were in flesh-colored tights or nude. He also ruled that there was no evidence to indicate that the pictures were taken at the Happy Bottom Riding Club. I knew then that I had 'em by the short hairs.

"By the time all of my witnesses finished, the Happy Bottom Riding Club sounded like a convent run by Mother Superior Pancho.

"You know, I always had a special knack for showmanship. I could take an ordinary-looking girl, use the right make-up, dress her in the right clothes, put her in the proper lighting and she'd come off looking like a raving fucking beauty. When the girl was naturally beautiful and knew how to carry herself, I could make her look like a real live candy cotton angel.

"January Smith was one of my natural beauties and she could make love to a man with her eyes and him standing clear across the room. She was just goddamn gorgeous.

"I put January on the witness stand looking like something out of a magnolia-shrouded antebellum mansion in Atlanta. That gal didn't walk to the stand, she floated with a trail of jasmine and magnolia clinging to everything she passed.

"January had those long, slim, sexy legs that drive men crazy and when she got on the stand she crossed them like a true lady but she flashed just enough flesh to attract everyone's undivided attention.

"I asked her if she understood that we had been accused of operating a whorehouse and she uttered a little cry of dismay. She looked like some painter's version of the pure virgin and conducted herself in the same manner. Von

Stroheim or Hughes couldn't have cast the part more perfectly.

"I caught Judge Beaumont eyeing January kinda' dreamily and I asked him if he thought that lovely lady looked like a prostitute to him. Without taking his gaze from January he shook his head no. Hot damn! We were on the downhill side now.

"Then I asked January if guys made passes at her or paid her money to make love to her and she was a perfect young Scarlett O'Hara in her shocked reaction to the question. Passes, yes, but to make love for money? Horrors, such a thought alone made her ill. I helped the innocent lamb from the witness stand and every eye in the room was on her as she melted into her seat. Hell, there wasn't a man on earth who would have condemned her for anything, she was so sweet and pure that they wanted to adopt her.

"When I nailed some of the lying assholes who claimed they bought sex at the ranch to the cross, coupled it with the impression that January made and the honest testimony of Walt Williams, I knew I had finally beaten the bastards.

"Took a couple more years for them to fuck around with appeals and such but they finally settled and awarded me $414,000 and some change. I told them to keep the change 'cause they probably needed it worse than I did.

"With that money I bought a spread up at Cantil, some more blooded horses, an airplane or two and started the Gypsy Springs Ranch. Times had changed, the Blow and Go guys were generals and corporate executives and the young pilots and navigators had cutie-pie wives and fast cars that would get them to the hot spots in Los Angeles or Vegas in a hurry so the place kinda fell on its ass.

"A couple of physical problems came along and I had to have my tits cut off and Mac and I fell apart and all of a sudden I was almost broke.

"That, my romantic little friend, is why I was on that goddamned horse in the canyon the other night—because I needed the lousy $68 they paid me. When we were talking about that earlier, I said something about it being so cold that I was freezing my tits off. I overlooked one little thing and now I remember that it seems to me that the whole world is computers and plastic and not much is real anymore.

"Rubber tits don't freeze, do they?"

EPILOGUE

The old woman on the magnificent mustang was suddenly aware of the signal for her ride to begin. She ignited the flammable end of her spear, kicked the mustang in the ribs, gathered the reins in her practiced, manicured fingers, and started the wild ride down the canyon wall. Like the charge of the goddamned Light Brigade.

She thundered through the group of actor-cowboys, planted her flaming spear among them, and galloped out of the range of the cameras. She knew that she had given a first-class performance. Pancho turned her horse and rode back among the stars and extras who were applauding.

"Goddamn assholes, now they know how me and Von Stroheim did it."